THE MAYS 16

Varsity Publications, Ltd.

Varsity Publications Ltd
Old Examination Hall
Free School Lane
Cambridge CB2 3RF

First published 2008 by Varsity Publications Ltd

ISBN 978-0-902240-38-4

Typeset in Baskerville by Erica Mena
Printed and bound by Y Lolfa Cyf. in Talybont, Wales

Original concept by Peter Ho Davies, Adrian Woolfson, Ron Dimant

A CIP catalogue record of this book is available from the British Library.

Further copies of this book and other titles in the series can be bought through most booksellers or direct from *Varsity Publications* at the address above or at:

http://mays.varsity.co.uk

Staff & Contributors

Guest Editor

Ian Patterson

Editors

Erica Mena | Deborah Smith

Managing Editor

Michael Derringer

Oxford Editor

Kristen Purdy

Poetry Readers

Tom Bailey | Alashiya Gordes | Lisa Jeschke | Madeleine Jones
Elisabeth Kershaw | Peter Morelli | Lucy Razzal
Emily Vasiliauskas

Fiction Readers

Trudy Ko | Emma Lowth | Zac Rose | Annabel Spearman
Hannah Thompson

Copyeditors

Maartje Geussens | Elizabeth Kershaw | Alexandra Lewis
Emma Lowth | David Tomlinson | Zhiying Tsjeng
Rebecca Wagner

Design and Layout

Erica Mena

Thanks to our college sponsors

CAMBRIDGE:

Clare Hall | Fitzwilliam College
Gonville & Caius College | Jesus College
Newnham College | Pembroke College
Queens' College | Trinity College

OXFORD:

Christ Church | Corpus Christi College
Jesus College | New College | Oriel College
St Hugh's College | St John's College
Trinity College | University College

CONTENTS

Introduction 1
by Ian Patterson

POETRY

Confessions of a Geek 5
by Will Crouch

Tonight 7
by Benjamin Morris

unpeeled 9
by Jane Han

poem 11
by Nadia Connor

Cradle Song 12
by Adam Crothers

After Rain 13
by Owen Holland

The Reporter Hotel 15
by Benjamin Morris

untitled 24
by Jane Han

november, here 26
by Marcelle Olivier

Shower 27
by Emily Tesh

Art

Tibo 57
by Naomi Grant

Hold 58
by Simone Kotva

Lonesome Mustang 59
by Cortland Rankin

Reds, Greens, & la Sacré-Coeur 60
by Cortland Rankin

blueyellowjazz 61
by Catherine Williams

PC160890b 62
by Ian Heames

Maria 63
by Beatrice Priest

Sarah 64
by Beatrice Priest

Kamuzu Stadium, Blantyre, Malawi, 2007 65
by Owen Holland

Sleeping Cat 66
by Megan Davies

Earth - Life - Peace 67
by Hazel Lambert

PROSE

Clarity 31
by Eley Williams

Camellia 39
by Ushashi Dasgupta

Enclosure 49
by Christopher Morley

China Shop 69
by Eley Williams

The Invention of Dice 81
by Benjamin Morris

Writing With Light 93
by Francesca Whitlum-Cooper

Starting and Stopping 105
by Eley Williams

Introduction

When John Lehmann's *New Writing* first appeared in 1936, its manifesto was deliberately low key; it would be 'devoted to imaginative writing, mainly of young authors' and did not 'intend to concern itself with literary theory, or the criticism of contemporaries'. It was, however, concerned to do what it could to use the power of the imagination to counter the growth of European fascism. Four years later, after four months of war, Cyril Connolly introduced the first issue of *Horizon* with the resigned lament that in a period that separated 'culture from life' it was impossible to expect to publish writing that was 'revolutionary in opinion or original in technique'. His standards were nevertheless 'aesthetic'. The *May Anthologies* have never been driven by revolutionary enthusiasms, and this year in particular the passion and muddle of 1968 has been so completely repackaged and re-presented as to turn the passing of 40 years into nostalgic cultural congratulation. But there's been so much written and spoken this year about the intrinsic connection between youth, novelty, revolution, change, fashion, politics and iconoclasm that it's hard not to wonder about these qualities as one reads through the selection. It's equally hard not to notice that these would not be the most helpful terms for thinking about these writings, the writings of 2008, which are frequently quite at home with themselves and bent on using that constructed poise to unsettle the reader in ways that are much more knowing about reading than they are overtly bothered about politics or stylistic innovation.

Writing, on the whole, it seems, goes on regardless of editorial postures. It goes on in all sorts of places, and with all sorts of aims and influences, but mainly it goes on in order to make new writing (to use Lehmann's phrase again, but depriving it of its editorial capital letters), because that's what its authors have to do. Its models come from all over the place, constituting a reflection of some kind of fiction zeitgeist that exists, as it always must, in hesitant dialectic between readers and writers and publishers and fractions of the world. Quietly and anonymously though these stories and poems have slipped onto my desk, they mostly show an awareness of a literary world relayed from the minds of editors, publishers, and taste-formers. Even perhaps from academics. On this showing, the revolutionaries, the literary experimentalists, the flaunting or reclusive iconoclasts, have all been routed. Or at least re-routed.

Which is partly as much as to say that the world is various, and I'm very glad that the responses to its variousness gathered and printed here are as accomplished and varied as they are. But I wonder what it would mean to say that 2008 may be a year of creative originality in prose, more than in poetry? So much, and so much of interest, has happened in British and American poetry (to speak no more widely than that) since 1968 that the Official English Version of what is possible, legitimate, desirable or fun to write in verse ought to have lost more of its power to shape the destiny of student writing. 'An enormous window morning and the wind, the beautiful desperation of a tree / fighting off strangulation'. Even the literary theory that John Lehmann excluded in 1936 might now suggest a greater range of possibilities. I'm able to say this unembarrassedly here and now because—despite being starved of nutrients—the poetry, too, in this anthology shows imagination and intellect and skill. And this is its elegant and proper function, to remind its readers (and I hope they are very many) of the undiminishing accomplishment, resourcefulness and aesthetic potential of new student writing.

Ian Patterson
Queens' College

POETRY

Confessions of a Geek

Will Crouch

How do I love thee? Here is my plight:
I cannot count the ways
For they are non-denumerably infinite.[1]
Even if I took all the particles in all the galaxies[2]
in all their temporal stages[3] since the beginning of Everything
I wouldn't have even got halfway.

How am I meant to say how I feel
When I am provided with a notation of such
limited expressive power?
No axiomatisation of my affection could ever be
sufficiently strong, consistent and complete.[4]
Yet I shall try:

You are not too dense; your mass is not too great.
Your bodily composition is mainly H2OK.
You've sent my visual system and my proprioception into
mutual confusion: for whilst
my eyes perceive two bodies, yet I feel only one.

We a binary star.
You, weaving the rainbow.[5]

You are my up quark when I'm a down quark; my charm quark
when I'm a strange quark.

---

[1] cf. Cantor 1891 for the proof why Browning's professed emotion amounts to little more than indigestion.

[2] 10^11 x 10^76 = 10^87

[3] 10^87 x 10^6 x 10^44 x (60 x 60 x 24 x 365) = 10^144

[4] Gödel 1931

[5] cf. Keats 1820 for an example of a real lack of imagination in this regard.

I the corpuscle, you the wave; we the photon. You the equal and
opposite reaction to my every action.

We the proof of quantum theory—ignore me and I no longer
live nor die.[6]
You weave the rainbow.

We two leptons with identical spin, which, even separated
to the other end of the galaxy
Can, faster than light, unmediated by Newtonian causation
and in defiance of Einstein's theory of General Relativity, any
amount of a priori philosophical speculation and every last
thread of common sense,
Alter the other just by a change in one's own state.

And so I come to this: my Copernican Revolution, my
transcendental deduction, the bedrock of my beliefs, my
epiphany running naked through the streets of Athens, the
Complete and Ultimate Universal One True Description of
Everything:[7]

$$i \alpha u$$

[6] Schrödinger 1931
[7] Einstein 1915; also cf. Putnam 1981 for an argument to the conclusion that this is impossible.

Tonight

Benjamin Morris

They should have made it a verb: *to*
night: to reach for a body;

alt., to come to the end of wandering,
to find harbor. So tonight we lay

coiled against each other, the breeze
grazing our skin after an evening

dimming swiftly through the window.
Had we lost this word for the hour outside,

would we still speak of it as a forest
yet to be charted, with your eye trailing

mine, the sound of your body changing shape
in the dark, dragging the shadows with it?

In the warmth my thoughts give way to water,
this room
composing itself anew

for you to wake into it—moonlight
etched on the mantle and the chairs

affixed to the wall, the bed
on the ceiling, rolling in the lap and tide of the sheets—

and were there no angels waiting
to save us from the storm, we would stay here

all night, praying, *deliver us to evil,*
for ours is the wreckage,
                    the body,
                      the cry.

unpeeled

Jane Han

on a day when the story of
two-column genocide makes the
page next to the Tiffany's ad

I arrive at the funeral of
a twice-acquainted relative
and spend time consoling

friends I do not know. dreams
don't come in color anymore
I am beside myself blowing

smoke into mirrors gazing
at twice-told lies of
circles and parallel lines.

I know the moon shines
nothing of its own and the
curves I trace on my lips converge

but I still believe
when night falls down undone
time will fold in my lap

only
this orange
to save us from carnage

holding round the world
its patient whole awakening
from its seed

the birth of now
untouched and
unpeeled

poem

Nadia Connor

where we had kissed&
held& my waist dipped in, handled, unhanded& not
untrue, where still we had not touched ourselves
the precedented copia of mess, the pathways sick
with roses& their unpursed lips like hearts
hysterical (but hearts unflamed) a half-heart hell
of answers unsought& deadly. what since
has gnarled us out of patterned hope for fears
to be upbraided& denied, for what once was
certain (or not un-so) to have belied us through&
through& owned our mortal tremor. in inchoate words
we form like pearls in mouths our rent contributors
to a too-sure world, we are become a hurting
in ourselves: *the only perfect is momentary, the only*
momentary is this, after all the troubled workings and
the bitten heart, too stung for service in so wild a
world. isolate words reaffirm my qualms. we
heed, or do not heed. & since we know
now what to expect, we'll not wheel round
the unflamed tree, the bitter lack, unstruck& deathly,
but yield dispersed& blank as paper to our absence
or upheaval; the artless, ardent, momentary fact.

Cradle Song

Adam Crothers

You would taste tamarind, and you would know
the leathery cool of whiskey, the give
of a door opened correctly; and now
and then, with only the slightest of coughs,
the wingspan of your heartbeat would increase,
borrowing the wind and skimming stones, once
cradled in the darks of olives, across
an impossibility of distance.

After Rain

Owen Holland

The sun did not shine, as such, but it did occasionally
break through the clouds & for a time, at least,
everything was safe & free & open.

The leaves look heavier & drooping
with the added weight of replenishment:
renewal is in the air, somehow thicker now;

the rain has disturbed the earth, made it
release its scent. We have tried to search
you out (for so long) but you have eluded us

& instantly my reserves are spent. I have no energy left
for the night, which will be with us soon
bringing the now common scuffles, brawls & fracas.

Little light of promises bleaks through the dark.
Your sturdy vessel makes some headway in the wind,
even though the dead have risen & walk the earth

unflinchingly. Make yourself plainer, effortless & un-
comprehending, because I cannot promise
to offer you hope – cannot promise anything

in *particular* – & the leaves have wrinkled now
in the wind and rain, shrivelling straight
from bud, almost. Their greenness revivified me

for two months: a short time, but finite.
At least it was finite. Scratch this out: 'Time
& the greatest occasions litter the noontide of our days.'

The blackened, unbreathable air envelops us
eventually & there is no stopping now, not at all,
not for anyone; we were told we were all

in this together – a great lie of unity,
a myth-making stab at the revolutionaries –
which remains urgently apparent, to some.

But this is not the blame game,
there are few games left which we can safely play.
And do not be shocked that I choose not to leave you

with any firm resolution or sense of an ending,
or be haughty & aghast that I desert you in your hour of need.

The Reporter Hotel

Benjamin Morris

i

At the desk a man dressed as a pickle
hands you your key,
says your dreams can be retrieved
between the hours of four and ten
daily or nightly, depending.
A cocktail struts by, sipping itself,
finds an escalator and
                                        falls up it.
There's a conference of birds
in the lobby—summer in Boca Raton
this year? Baton Rouge?—their lustrous wings
shimmering in the half light of the lounge,
like your bags, leaping now
to your hands as the pickle
takes a call. You take a breath,
a mint, begin the long walk home.

ii

How's your trip? the flytrap asks,
yawning, sniffing for flies.
Fine, your face shrugs, your coat
slipping to a puddle at your feet.
The minibar is full, but there's
nothing to say, nothing
to do now that you're here.
The revolution is being televised,
people out on the streets of some city
walking as if suddenly they had
nowhere to go—*do you want to lie down?*
the plant asks, but no, the thought
is too much, what you really need
is a swim

iii

in the lake of her mind,
where she is waiting
with pineapple cut with a sword,
towels baked in honey,
rosewater waves and the softest
murmur of a maillot—*Excuse us,*

iv

sir, calls the desk, *There's a problem*
with your room. There appears
to be someone thinking in it.
Thank you, sir. Straightaway.
Don't wait, the flytrap whispers,
draped loosely over a vine
like the shirt you left on the shore
when you found her—out,
out the door
down the hall
past the ice
and the maid
from whose cart
you pluck three
tightly bottled fantasies.
—But why the Sahara? Well,
there's a run in the meerkat
and besides, the elevator still giggles
at each press of its— six floors down,
past the gym
and the spa
and the pool
and the zoo
and the jail
and you find

v

the shop, two penguins, and the news.
On the screen a mimic of headlines
run slowly after each other, the magazines
are in bloom, and the papers lay
neatly folded as maps:
words puffing merrily as tugs across the page,
where the world is not flat,
just rectangular, and the poets sing
of the ink-dark sea. *We know what*
you need to know, reads a sign
on the door. *Back in an hour.*
But you don't have time, you don't have—

vi

one bauble under glass shines *me! me!*
and another laughs, *I rattle*
when you give me a shake.
How
to choose? Your sister likes animals
with the names of cities:
Cleveland, she has. Or is it
Portland. Oakland. All these lands
so far away as to curve in the mind
like a lens, their names with no edges
to grasp—and until *she* arrives,
answers folded gently in her bag,
it's no use. You wish you could

vii

hold her,
ask her to help you
remember.

viii.

No messages at the desk.
No telephones in sight.
No exits or entrances anymore,
just doors, but plenty to keep you
awake—the prison break, revolving
bars, fire swallowing men on stage,
but no one to tell it to—so why
bother? Your meeting's not till late
(where's the men's? your key? your—)
and surely they're still searching
your room. You hope they find it,
the sign on the desk that says
In case of fire, burn. —But where
is she? Distant, you look around the lobby
to make sure she hasn't just slipped
out of sight, around a corner, always
one step ahead even when she's not
running—*Time is a marvellous thing*
to kill, the pickle offers. *You never*
have to hear it scream.

And now,
say the televisions overhead,
snow is falling all over the country,
all over Rockland. Raceland. Graceland.

ix

The Number 12 is tending the bar,
pouring tonic from its spout
and stirring ice with its stick—
a Sidecar for yourself, double whiskeys
for the penguins and a Gibson for the desk—

and as it glides it grouses
where's that lazy 7? Leaning,
no doubt, against the wall out back,
holding a smoke, cursing the day

it took this job—the bruise and the burn of it,
the ash that falls like snow.
                                        Only ever a parade
of shoes walking through these doors,
running endlessly
                    away from themselves,
              looking to find something they won't find
         here, someone meant to be ordering gin,
who's come and gone
                         already last night,
who collected herself and her regrets
from the desk,
                    hailed a cab,
                    stepped inside,
                    closed the door, couldn't
         look back, couldn't
remember your

untitled

Jane Han

i.

spring.
those
hands
that sting cheeks
with dotted streaks
of cherry blossoms

ii.

winter.
wrap warm and mastic
around five pencils
as we wait
single-filed
and barefoot
before our
squatting
father

the felled pitter
of slender pine
aligning slender
against the floor
as he carves
strong and clean
bold even points
balming
those
weathered
hands
with
spiced wood.

november, here

Marcelle Olivier

and now i see you everywhere:
in the tracks of ice, whispers caught, fish, a motion
like a wave. i am found staring, and taken in.

it is harrowing, the shedding of the sun
on winter afternoons; watchers see the leaves
crack and curl; birds eating fast at the dropped corns.

i see you, sitting with them, a live wire spun
like a strand of glint, an invisible web
holding you afloat to the skinny wind. once again

i am found staring, and taken in, like a child.
your ash-yellow hair at the market. coarse
ringlets at the cinema, bouncing to your shoulders.

everyone is wearing you like a fashion:
like wools and felts are seasonal luxuries this year;
soon every lock will be frozen, see, everywhere.

boats do not move; fake fires glimmer in the water.
it lies, and the reeds play on like a confidence, to
the breeze, to the rambler-marksman's winter-walk.

there is your untidy fringe leaning to the pharmacist,
his mouth close to yours, and you are breathing.
i see your head in a hat at the buses, haloed fumes;

a late butterfly awkwardly flung to convections.
i see you everywhere, not waiting for me, and the season
an open grate, raw embers for a reading; a motion

like a playful trot on a polished floor; glowing
across. far away i hurt myself for you. everywhere
i am caught staring, and taken in, far from you.

Shower

Emily Tesh

I leave some evidence that I've been past:
a line of fading kissprints on the glass.

PROSE

Clarity

Eley Williams

ONE EYE OPENED. After a minute, it experimented with winking.

No need to attempt anything else just yet, the winker reasoned. Sue had been woken by the bang of the door, signalling that she was alone in the flat; for whom, she submitted to the ceiling-plaster, would I be getting up? For what?

Perhaps I will never get up from this settee.

That actually wouldn't be so bad; certainly easier than climbing to my feet. Opening the other eye, moving the arms, all that business with the knees—she imagined that never moving from the settee, never ever, would be far simpler. I will get a little thirsty, get very thirsty, I will pass out on this settee and then crumble into nutrient-rich, Eco-friendly mulch. If you filmed all that and played it back at ten times the speed, Sue thought, the whole process wouldn't take too long at all. The film would start, her eye would open and *Poofft*!!!, just a dusty settee.

She would change her answer-phone message to explain where she was to all her friends. The council might draw up a petition to move her, to build a bypass through her, but she wouldn't budge.

She swiveled the eye. There was something lying by her head on the settee's armrest.

Maybe if I stayed on this settee forever, Sue continued, my bones might knit and calcify into just one big bone so I *could* never move, only tip and pivot about. My eyelashes might dovetail-joint together and never be prized apart. My skin would become as one with the leather of the settee, and all that would remain would be my eyebrows, and the earth would crawl up over me, and archaeologists would dig me up in a million years' time, and gasp, and wonder if we were all like that a million years ago.

Staying on the settee forever suddenly felt like a lot of responsibility.

Her eye realised the thing by her head was a note, pinned right into leather of the armrest.

'Sorry about last night.
I left a sandwich on the side. Hope you like pickle!
See you later.—B'

The eye winked again.

Had B told her to sleep on the settee? She couldn't remember. Maybe she offered to sleep there, hoping she would get lost down the back of it. 'About £1billion is lost, or lying idle, in the UK's 24.7 million households'. The fact blurted out into her head from some long-forgotten Trivial Pursuit card. *Fascinating.* On average, then, how much spare change might be down the back of this specific settee right now? Let me try and work it, Sue thought. That figure, minus this figure, carry the three. Carry the three in the alm-bowl of my head, hold it there, go go go,

(Sue isn't entirely sure how much is in a billion. She knows one thousand billion used to be called a 'billiard', however, which she's pretty sure is a better sleight of knowledge.)

The eye focused on the wristwatch thwacking out the seconds next to her face. She felt it was safer to check her own watch rather than the clock on the wall; she wasn't entirely sure that Time in B's sitting room wouldn't be quicker, or slower, or counting in different numbers, or something.

Quarter past twelve, said her watch. The quality of light through the window meant it must be a quarter past twelve in the afternoon. Good call. Detective skills, interpreting data; a quarter past twelve p.m. She had slept too long.

Sue read the note again; it was, after all, the last thing she would ever read before she became mere *Poofft*!!! dust on a settee. She reckoned that she owed it to herself to get a full understanding of what the note was trying to tell her.

Her favourite word on the note was 'pickle'. It was fun. The exclamation mark made it even more fun. Pick-le. It was a pizzicato word. Pickle: a pink tickle that prickled at a fickle pucker I plucked at, chuckling, truculent. Pickle pickle pickle.

Given that it was now a quarter past twelve p.m., the note could either be offering her a late breakfast or an early lunch. Not a very time-specific thing, a sandwich. She supposed the mealtime for which it was intended depended entirely upon what was *within* the sandwich; if it was an egg and bacon and pickle sandwich, for example, it was almost certainly a breakfast sandwich. One of those All-Day Breakfast sandwiches. Can you actually break your fast *all day long*, Sue wondered. That sounded very impractical. Maybe you could have your egg and bacon and pickle sandwich kind of blended, blent, into a soup that you could carry around with you all day – like, via an IV drip or something. 'Via IV'. Ivy Via-Drip, a daughter of the landed gentry.

Breaking your fast all day is oxymoronic, thought Sue, and her eye smiled.

All you need to eat a sandwich is a hand. And a mouth, one presumes. So, basically, B has left a sandwich out for me to show I am not supposed to open any drawers in B's house, not supposed to get my fingerprints on any of his crockery. His cutlery. Crockery and cutlery: also lovely words. We have plenty of time before I become as one with the settee, so let's pause and dwell on those words, thought Sue. Crockery, cutlery, cuttlefish in a rockery. Rookery. Cuttleryfish.

A gust of wind sounded outside, and Sue saw lines of rain nuzzling at the window. She imagined the world beyond this room, the street B had stepped out into, a street bulbous and shiny with umbrellas. She thought of all the water that must have hit B in little pieces when B slammed the door and stepped into B's garden, leaving her alone in the flat.

'I left a sandwich on the side'. Why did B phrase it like that? That was a statement of fact, not an offer. It said, *I have done something specific with a sandwich at one time or another. Not for you, not for anyone: I just did it, and now you're going to know all about it.* And what does B mean by 'side'? Everything has a 'side'. Chairs, tables, rooms, stories, wars. Which side did B mean? Will I ever find my sandwich, Sue wondered. Her eye rolled a little, without her thinking about it.

'Hope you like pickle!', the note said. Not, *Do you like pickle?* or, *I've put pickle in your sandwich, is that alright?* B was clearly thoughtless to her preferences vis-à-vis pickle. True, the 'Hope you like' was considerate, but the final exclamation mark made the phrase look like it was either trying too hard to please, or else it was a joke. *I hope you like pickle, BECAUSE I'VE ONLY GOT JAM AND BAKING SODA IN MY CUPBOARD!*, that is what the exclamation mark said. It was manic.

I Hope You Like Pickle!!!!!!!!!!!!!!!!!!!!!!!!!!!!!

And what did B actually mean by 'pickle'? Pickle, what a pickle. Some kind of chutney, was it? A piccalilli (piccalilli, Piccadilly, peccadillo, armadillo)? Or a gherkin, a *cornichon*, that cucumber-knobble kind of pickle they eat by the jar in documentaries about Poland, and slice up and put into handburgers over here. Sorry, hamburgers. Americans call gherkins 'pickles', don't they? Don't you have an American aunt, B? B certainly has American trainers. Converse. Sue can see them, with her eye, under the armchair opposite her settee. Have your trainers' native Americanisms inked up your bloodstream and into your mouth and your writing fingers? Did you write 'pickle' as an American? Did I fall out with an American last night? Me on the settee, you on the armchair? The chair made for your arms.

She looked at the note again.

Sue notices B has left her no drink. B wants Sue to desiccate. B wants her kidneys to hiccup and grunt, then wilt inside her.

The eye closed.

The eye opened, and scaned the note again.

'Left' a sandwich. Didn't 'place', didn't 'bequeath' it unto me it with due reverence and solemnity: B discarded it, dropped it and didn't bother to pick it up and now I, Sue, have to eat it, like one of those dogs at Henry VIII's court who must scrounge off the banquet floor for discarded gristle and bone. Henry VIII was a big guy; those scrounging dogs can't have eaten very much. *I didn't need the sandwich, I could do without it.* That's what the note meant. *You and the sandwich will get on famously.*

You want to torture me with ambiguity, B, Sue thought.

Her eye ran over the first line of the note. She couldn't even say for sure what had happened last night. Could she think of a word for it? 'Argument' made it sound too rational; 'fight' made it seem too violent; 'spat' made it sound petty. It was all of these things and none of these things. All she could remember was that it had started when B could not find the TV remote, and it had ended—not as planned, with B and Sue together, asleep, ampersand-shaped in a bed—with Sue waking up alone on this settee reading this note with her one open eye.

You couldn't even be bothered to write your full name. B. Buh. -B-B-B: A string of half-butterflies. 'B': a fat woman in profile. A fat woman with no head and no arms or legs. Your name is sick and a little bit depraved, B.

Would there be crusts on the bread? Does B wish I had curlier hair? And would it be a normal sandwich, or a club sandwich? A bloomer roll? Bloomers are some kind of expansive undergarments, Sue knew. Blooming, budding. Isn't a 'bloomer' a mistake? A bloomin' error. Do I mean blooper? A blooper roll? I'm going to develop a gluten intolerance right NOW, decided Sue: I'm going to close my eye, wish myself dark in the face, and tolerate gluten no more.

Her eye widened suddenly. £40 WORTH OF SPARE CHANGE COULD, ON AVERAGE, BE DOWN THE BACK OF THIS SETTEE. I COULD BUY THE WHOLE STREET SOME SANDWICHES OF THE HIGHEST QUALITY ENTIRELY INDEPENDENTLY OF B.

Something quite sinister about the final 'See you later' too. It's the full stop. *I will see you later. We shall not meet; I will see you, and that will be the end of it.*

Sue opened her other eye.

Sue got up.

Sue shook all the cutlery out of the drawers in B's flat. She turned the taps on and started the dishwasher, the tray stacked with soap and the door wedged open. She poured some orange juice, which was not left out for her, into a pot-plant. Sue put the pot-plant in the microwave. Sue made tea with all B's teabags in the sink, with half a bag of sugar to taste; when she found the TV remote down the back of the settee, she put it in the fish-tank. With a pair of Converse shoes. She unplugged the fridge and put the toaster in the bath. This shouldn't hurt B, Sue thought as she did it: B'll notice a toaster in the bath, won't B, before B starts running it? Sue chucked all the crumbs out of the toaster before putting it in the bath, because who could imagine anything worse than a bath-full of crumbs?

Sue put on her coat, opened the door and switched off the light. She paused, then switched the light back on again.

Sue went out into the rain in the front garden, and shut the door behind her.

The sandwich lay untouched on the tabletop, a new note propped beside it. Strictly speaking it was the same note flipped over, but with a new message written on the back.

Dear B,
It's OK.

Camellia

Ushashi Dasgupta

IT WAS THE KIND OF PLACE where they built pawn shops next to betting stations, and thought even God's business card could be printed in neon. Water dripped from air-conditioners and old ladies wearing boaters hosed the drains, leaving oily puddles on the street. There were sheets of bamboo scaffolding which seemed to grow out of the ground, out of windows and holes in the faces of buildings where brick had been lost. Everything was thick—thick with petrol and breath, thick with hurry. Except now.

Natalie put the thermos flask next to the cash register, checking, by way of habit, whether it was still warm. She brushed her fingers against the metal once, too quickly to feel anything; then again, for longer. The ends of her pale blue ballet flats just touched the line between two floor tiles. She could feel the warmth of her hands as they lay on her stomach. All was silent here and she had become used to it, much as a construction worker probably gets used to noise. The four of them never noticed, but they were all going slowly deaf. The silence outside meant they never needed to hear more than whispers—they never faced the usual screaming day streets, for their flower shop opened late at night, run by four people who were losing the use of their ears.

Natalie saw the door open before she registered the fluttery ringing of the bell. She liked that door—the top half was glass, and filtered copper light from the lampposts to their floor. They could also watch their customers-to-be peer inside while pretending not to notice at all.

Trammy was waving a paper bag in Natalie's face.

"Bought some McDuck's from the death district," she said. "McChicken and fries for you."

"Thanks. Death district thriving?"

Trammy shrugged, picking up the small cash register from the table and setting it on the floor.

"Not really. Pretty quiet." She took out the food, the napkins, two flat straws. She had pushed down all of the plastic bubbles on the lid of her drink. "Only the McD's was open—no queue and I didn't even feel guilty about taking five ketchups."

Natalie lifted up her drink and wiped the pool of condensation off the table. "Do you want the extra?"

"Yes," Trammy said. "That good with you?"

Natalie nodded.

They ate for a few minutes, Trammy digging around in a low cupboard with half a chip in her hand, Natalie contemplating the way ketchup soaked a tissue in rings.

"Bad news, though," Trammy said suddenly.

"What is it?"

"The chalk is gone."

"*No.*"

"Afraid yes. At least it was there a little while."

A few nights ago, Trammy and Natalie had been walking towards the death district together. It was a few streets away—uneven rows of low shops with no doors, shaded by off-white awnings, selling coffins and orange funeral flowers. Nothing else. They had been walking down the silent road—no need for the pavement when there were no cars—when they came across some graffiti written in chalk across the concrete. *Hey man/Jaws was never my scene/And I don't like Star Wars.* Trammy and Natalie had stood quietly for a moment, the toes of their shoes just below the words, Natalie's white skirt blowing a little.

"Thanks for getting the food," Natalie said now, folding the wrapper of her finished burger. "I'm sorry you had to go by yourself."

"Oh, hey," Trammy said. "The district isn't half bad."

"But it's not really pleasant at night."

Trammy made a sound through her nose. Natalie thought for a moment about the walk from the district to their flower shop; the faint tapping of shoes against subway steps. Dreamily, she told Trammy that their latest order of roses had been delivered that night.

This bouquet was too loud. Natalie looked at it, her head tilted slightly away from the flowers. She frowned a little, leaned forward, and leaned back again. Then she took out a dark red carnation. It seemed to peel away from the bouquet, its stem arching in her hand.

Trammy yawned. She pushed her thick, black-rimmed reading glasses to the tip of her nose and scrutinised Natalie with uncovered eyes.

"Did you not sleep well?" Natalie said.

"Mm?"

"Why are you tired?"

Trammy told her she was not tired. She had woken up at nine, having slept at eleven that morning. She went back to her book.

It was unusual, Natalie thought, that so few people had visited the shop to this point tonight. It was quiet. Trammy (or one of the others, when it was their shift) was usually gliding from corner to corner, Natalie to the opposite ones, gathering things they thought might appeal to each suited man and stranger knocking the sides of the doorway in his anxiety, Trammy reciting the list of flower symbols she had invented for business purposes ("You can't go wrong with yellow freesia. They mean innocence and pure love. No bad intentions at *all*.").

"But then again," Natalie said, half to herself, "it is a Thursday."

Trammy loudly turned a page.

"Yeah, business is slow tonight." She tapped the book with her nail. "You know, this is good."

The door opened. Natalie saw the shadow of the person spread across the floor before hearing the bell. She saw Trammy pull her glasses off her nose and rest them on her chin.

"Hey. I'm Trammy, this is Nat. Can we help?"

Natalie cast the pirouette carnation next to the cash register and looked up.

The customer, she could see, was considering Trammy and blinking—the reading glasses hanging from Trammy's ears, the frayed school leavers' hoodie, the copy of *Sense and Sensibility* in one hand.

"Natalie," Natalie said.

He was wearing jeans and a blazer, and had hooded eyes and thick brows. He looked tall.

"Hi. I'm glad you're still open."

"Course we're open. We're open all night. Good thing you didn't try and come during the day. All you'd have seen is a closed sign and an old woman smoking on the pavement up front." Trammy pointed in the general direction of the door.

"I'm looking for flowers."

"Well, good." Trammy stood up. "What kind?"

Now that Trammy was on her feet, Natalie saw that the man did not seem quite so tall. How deceptive.

As Trammy sashayed past Natalie, she whispered, I wonder who they're *for*!

Natalie turned her pocket inside out. A tissue floated to the ground. She picked it up swiftly.

The man was looking around at the bouquets of arranged flowers lined across tables; at the clusters of unsorted lilies, dahlias and gladioli kept in buckets on the floor. Natalie watched as he shook his head.

"What kind?" he repeated. "I don't know. Maybe you both could help me decide?"

Trammy threw *Sense and Sensibility* down beside a pot of sunflowers.

"Right. Why do you need them? Who are they for?"

"Trammy," Natalie said.

Trammy opened her mouth in a delicate 'o' and widened her eyes, her black liner stretching.

"Just curious. And anyway, we need to know, don't we, Nat? Then we can help you,"—she nodded primly at the man —"find the right thing."

He cleared his throat.

"Well."

He paused. Natalie stared at her feet, noticing how she'd kept one a little behind the other.

"Mm, I see. We get a lot of customers who go there. You know, down in that general direction." She pointed in the direction of the neighbourhood brothel and beamed at him. "One of the main reasons we're around, you know. The men just come here first, pick up some flowers—"

Natalie's hand rose to Trammy's elbow and swatted at it.

"What?" Trammy looked at Natalie, then peered at the man. "Come to think of it, you are a little young. What are you, twenty-five? They're usually middle-aged. Mid-life crisis, you know. On the way to work every evening, I come across all sorts of black Jaguars and red Maseratis and dark blue BMWs parked a safe distance away. If you follow those hiding cars, you find that they make a secret path to our shop."

All Natalie heard were small, subtle bones cracking in her hands. She looked down and saw how tightly they were clasped, waiting for the belated sound of the bell to reach her as he left the shop. When it did not come, she glanced up.

"I'm not going—there," the man was saying. His eyes were fixed on the closest pile of flowers. "These are nice."

Natalie's head turned quickly.

"Camellia," she said.

"Camellia?"

"Camellia. Do you not want a bouquet we've already arranged? We have one here with tulips, white tulips, and hyacinths. Or this one—" (standing on tiptoe, pointing behind him quite randomly) "—lots of yellows. Mainly yellows."

"They're too fancy," Trammy said. "Too fancy, right?"

"A bit. But even if I don't buy one of those arranged bouquets, if I chose them myself, would it be all right if you still wrapped the flowers up? With the ribbons, or the string that goes curly if you run it over a scissor-blade."

"Of course it's all right," said Trammy. "We are florists, not the supermarket. We wouldn't throw a couple of gerberas at you that were tied together with masking tape or an elastic band."

"That's good to know."

"Camellia is lovely," Natalie said feebly.

He nodded. She saw it was a slow, rhythmic nodding, which seemed to go on for a long time. He was staring at the cash register—it still lay where Trammy had deposited it, on the floor.

"Well, I suppose they're for the girl I am seeing. The lady I'm seeing, I guess."

Natalie had seen men buy last minute flowers for their girlfriends many times, and they were typically matter-of-fact. Maybe a little nervous, spinning their credit cards on the tips of their nails, absently tearing stray petals from daisies (whether they were charged for the damage or not depended on Trammy's mood). Switching off their mobile phones or reading the headlines on the scraps of newspaper Trammy and Natalie used to wrap the flowers. *Fed-Express wins Grand Slam. Ancient Temple Found in Peru.* But they didn't answer Trammy's usual question like this, as if they were trying to step on early grass without feeling dewdrops on the edges of their feet.

"So what does she look like?" Trammy asked.

"She—she has black hair?"

"Camellia," Natalie said with deliberation, "does not go with that colour."

Trammy stared at her.

"It doesn't. It definitely does not."

She did not know what she was talking about, and Trammy took no time in pointing this out. Trammy then took it upon herself to tell the man that camellia symbolised fidelity, innocence and pure love.

"As does baby's breath," she said, promptly adding them to the bouquet.

"They symbolise the same thing?"

"A similar thing. Layers of meaning, you see. Our art is all about subtlety. Don't you agree, Natalie?"

"Well—yes, of course."

A few moments' silence.

"Yes, of course," Natalie repeated quietly.

"That's nice," he said.

Another pause.

"Surely they can't be very happy, the people who must come here," he said at last. His hands were deep in his pockets, and the sleeves of his blazer seemed to be swallowing him. "Unhappy people, stopping by here before going—down the street."

"Well, we've been here for a long time, and it isn't just unhappiness. Trust me. Not from what we've seen," Trammy said.

"No," said Natalie. "It is."

He looked down at his watch.

"I'm early," he said. "She won't be at her place for another hour."

He must have stepped out of his apartment too soon, Natalie thought; too eager to leave, too unsure of what flowers he needed. He could not have been seeing the woman for long.

"Would you like some tea, then, as you've got time? We have some here," Trammy said.

"Tea?"

"Yes. We have some here." Trammy drew out a wicker chair and slid cups to the table. "There's no sugar, milk or lemon, though. Just so you know."

He accepted, glancing down at his watch again. Soon they were seated around the little table, Natalie offering around biscuits on which the grains of sugar had started to melt. He told them he was married.

Natalie looked down at the biscuit held across her two palms, and knew this was not unexpected.

"I wish we had some bourbon creams," she found herself saying.

"My wife is in Sweden. Rebecca."

She had been there for three weeks so far. She called him any time during the day, before or after work, whenever the whim took her; never at night though her jetlag warranted it, as she knew he'd be asleep. She also believed in letters, pressing the pen down so hard that he could feel ridges on the back of each postmarked envelope, sending him fortune cookies and menus in Swedish.

"A letter arrived this morning. *Isn't it strange, my dear? It's a sign that appears everywhere, but with different wording, depending on the country you're in. 'Do not use the elevator in case of fire'. 'If there is a fire do not use the lift'. Shoddy punctuation is the only thing we all seem to have in common.* Shoddy punctuation; elevators or lifts. She's—the kind of person who likes cats, and rehearses what she's going to say before leaving a voicemail." He put down his cup. Natalie saw him run his finger around its chipped base.

"Even when she's calling you?" she asked in spite of herself.

"Sometimes, I think."

It was an unconscious thing for her, he said. Compulsive. They had been married for two years.

"Don't you want tea, Nat?" Trammy asked.

"Thanks, no."

He was looking into the cup on the table. Trammy refilled it with tea.

"Thank you." He drank some. "I feel I have to explain myself. I mean, I'm on the way to Kaya's place. She's not—it isn't like I'm one of those men who come here to pick up flowers before going down the *street*."

Natalie shook her head. Of course he was not. And there was no way, no way, that she would help him find flowers. She—

He told them about Kaya. She was tiny, he told them; really, really small. She was collaging her ceiling, ripping the cuttings apart whenever she wasn't happy with the results, throwing the shreds from her balcony.

Natalie stood up.

"That's nice," she said stiffly.

"Yes," Trammy said, "she sounds amazing. Don't think about anything until Rebecca comes back. Now, about these flowers."

"What?"

"The flowers. Camellia, I think we decided, and baby's breath?"

The teacups were then put down, the pink one, the green one with white polka dots, and Trammy and the man started going through the flowers in each red bucket. Natalie watched them for a while, finding that her breath wasn't regular.

"Those," she said, pointing at the bouquet, "you can't buy those. They aren't—they aren't nice. This isn't good. Please don't."

"Natalie. These are nice flowers. Be quiet," Trammy said.

"They aren't."

"I think Kaya will like them," he said. "I hope so."

Natalie saw he was thinking, looking at them. Thinking, perhaps, what vase Kaya would put them in, and where she would put the vase; on her yellow breakfast table, next to the window and newspapers and bimonthly magazines. She had probably taped her charcoal drawings to the living room wall. Would she trim the corners when they began to fray?

"I don't know what I should do," he was saying.

"When is Rebecca coming back, anyway? Next month? That's really too long," said Trammy.

A pause. He took out his wallet. It was black.

"How much?"

He handed the money to Natalie. She sat down on the floor to work the cash register, feeling it whir against her shins before she heard it.

"Your change."

"Thank you."

Natalie felt her throat hurt.

"I like camellia," she told him. She wrapped up the flowers and tagged them with an illegally reproduced photo of two romantic comedy celebrities (who would search for copyright infringers in sleeping streets, anyway?). "And I don't know what you should do. But," she said, "if you decide to choose between Kaya and Rebecca, you'll at least have one of them, whoever you choose. You won't be—well—" She trailed off weakly.

"That's true." He left.

"And the shop will always be open," Trammy said as she settled down with her book, "to provide service and flowers to whichever girl. Don't you think this Rebecca sounds like a daffodil sort?" She looked for her reading glasses. "The art, Natalie, of romance."

Natalie nodded. She was standing small and still against a shelf, staring at a poster on the wall and noting, again and again in a string of repetitions, that it was crooked. It was crooked. It was crooked.

Rebecca and Kaya—for a few minutes Natalie had wanted the man to forget about them both. But then she thought, maybe the lives of strangers were more important than that. That was what they did at the shop, after all—Trammy and Natalie herself and the other two who worked there. They listened to these unfamiliar people and gently set them on their way to something that might give them a month's happiness, or so. The four of them were there to create things for other people, and their own lives were supposed to remain small. As she poured some lukewarm tea from the thermos she felt she could hear the lights above her. They were humming.

Enclosure

Christopher Morley

Definition: *Causewayed Enclosure.* A type of monument comprising one or more circuits of interrupted ditch. Function remains unclear, though a ritual or ceremonial role is likely. Alternatively, the presence of human remains may suggest their use in excarnation…

2*008AD*. WHEN ADAM OAK'S mother died of breast cancer he didn't cry. He didn't shout or scream or get all upset and need consoling. No, he was too old for all that. Instead he built himself an enclosure. It took him a full week to dig the ditches. There were fifteen of them, one for every year of his life. When he'd first started off, there was going to be just a single circular ditch, with the earth piled up along the outside edge. But then he stopped—he'd only just dug his spade in—and really thought about it. And the more he thought about it, the less he liked the idea of a single ditch and bank. It was too suffocating. He wanted to be in charge of the enclosure, not the other way round. This was going to be *his* place. He needed to be able to stand in the middle and see out in every direction. To enter and exit any way he pleased. Being funnelled through the same gap was not part of the plan. The answer was simple: divide and conquer. He set about marking out the length of each ditch segment, all about three metres long by a metre wide. Then at 15:32 on the day of his mother's funeral, Adam Oak started to dig.

The surrounding countryside was chalkland given over to pasture, and the site itself was a patch of waste ground on a low hill behind the family home. The area was lightly wooded and the nearest village was Stow, several miles away, so you didn't have to worry too much about intruders. The digging was hard work. He went down about a metre into the topsoil with each ditch. They could always be made deeper if need be. His shovel crunched away at the unresponsive earth, its mail of flint glancing aside every other lunge, and on into the underlying chalk. He piled the spoil up along the outside edges, careful to leave each of the fifteen causeways clear. More than clear. Pristine. You could have piled it up on the inside of course, but then there would be no way of seeing the contents of the ditches. There were so many things to consider when building yourself an enclosure—he tossed up another shovel-full—odd things that would never have occurred to you before you started digging.

As he worked he sang and uttered prayers. They weren't prayers to God. Who believed in that old shite? It was okay to be spiritual though. Spiritual was different. Odds on there must have been something out there. Something god-like, if not an actual god. So it was best to just pray to the universe at large, to everything and nothing, let whatever was out there tune-in if it felt the urge or fancied a good laugh. Who knows, perhaps humans and god-like things were on a more even keel. He prayed that the weather stayed nice. It had been a fantastic spring, weather-wise. The warmest on record. Digging in the rain wouldn't have been any fun. He prayed that his father would stop drinking. Since his mother had fallen ill, he'd drunk more and more. In fact when the hell had he last been sober? It was hard to tell by now. So that was it then. Both parents gone.

He prayed that he had the patience to finish the enclosure. He was terrible for starting things and never finishing them. She always used to tell him that. Pretty much the last thing she said. Wasn't it? Hopefully. But anyway this *was* important. He had no idea why. But it was. And it would have been important to her that he finished it. It was partly her enclosure anyway. If she hadn't gone and fucked right off like that then he'd probably never have created it. Never even dreamed up the stupid idea in the first place. Fifteen ditches, one for every year of the life she'd given him, one for every year she'd been there for him. Well, that was only fourteen really. The last one he'd pretty much been there for her; in the hospital, at home next to her bed, talking calmly as if everything was just fine. Would have given anything to be able to scream. To have huffed and puffed and blown the whole fucking house down.

With the start of each new ditch he racked his brain for relevant memories. There were none before the age of three. Not really. So he invoked some of his old baby pictures. They sat festering away in a box, a monstrous box full of dusty albums and dog-eared packets, buried under a load of other useless old junk in the loft. He forced himself back into those tiny exposed heads. Unable to control his bowels properly. Unable to feed himself; needing a tit shoved into his greedy face. Circle of life or what! He giveth with one tit, taketh away with the other. After the age of three though, the memories came thick and fast. Days out; birthdays; first days at school; arguments; holidays; make-ups; injuries; Christmases. Out they spewed, right up until ditch fifteen.

He didn't sleep that much during construction. Didn't need to. It's not like he dug non-stop or anything. He did do a lot, obviously, but then he also did a lot of praying and a lot of thinking. There was a great deal of thinking involved in a place like this, in an enclosure. Thought was the foundation. It probably sounded weird to people who'd never dug themselves an enclosure before, but the banks and ditches weren't the half of it. The real stuff was in your head.

He'd set himself up a little two-man tent in the interior and filled it with snacks and drink. He napped there every so often, when his back ached too much for him to lift the shovel. Still went back to the house every night for dinner, mainly because his father was never in any fit state to feed himself. Probably would've left the hob on and burnt the place down. He needed to be with him as well, just a few moments in the day. To sit with him, the silent shadow in front of the TV, glugging away disinterestedly.

A week and a half after his mother's funeral, digging was complete. He climbed a nearby tree and gazed down on his enclosure for the first time. It was a bit larger than expected, perhaps ten metres or so across. Wasn't exactly circular either, but then fair play it wasn't too bad. Looked like a ring of sausages. There were five trees dotted around the interior. They were only young and their trunks were not much wider than Adam's grip. He slunk back down the much larger tree and spent a couple of hours hacking the tops off them, trimming away the branches and sharpening the tops into stakes. This was the most awkward thing of all, because you had to stretch up above your head and slash upwards until there was no blood left in your arms. After a solid week of digging that was hard work. He did it all the same though. Then, satisfied that pikes were more in keeping with his enclosure, he returned to the treetop perch.

This time it was perfect, the symmetry of it. How your eye could follow it round and round like a segmented tyre. How there was no beginning or end. Leaving the perch again he re-entered between ditches six and seven; between the seaside holiday spent in the penny arcades and on the beach eating ice-cream, between that and the time he'd broken his arm and mum had made him a special 'get better' hat which helped him get better much faster than the doctors said. He walked into the centre and scanned around. From the inside the enclosure looked different. Completely different to what it looked like from outside, from the perch. From there it had *looked* safe and it had *looked* inviting and it had *looked* like his. But from inside it *felt* it. It *felt* all of those things. It even smelt and sounded like them. It tasted. He was proud of the ditches, his ditches, which gaped like open mouths whispering into the dusk. Then he unzipped his flies and walked anti-clockwise around them firing a short burst of piss into each one.

The enclosure had been up and running for several weeks before the day of the glass run. By this time the clean cut edges had begun to weather. The earth no longer looked sculpted as it slipped into the cuts. Instead it looked cracked and pitted beneath a skin of muck; natural, as if somehow ditches had always been there; timeless, as if somehow they always would. The leaves and other crap that had gathered in the bases were slowly turning to sludge. He made his way back through the trees, across the brook, over the fence and down the garden. As he approached the house, the bags and crates were caked like plaque around the outside wall. Their contents were all the same: empty bottles. The process was familiar, achingly so. His father spawned them, he collected them up before they multiplied like bacteria. Then he dumped them all in one reeking clutch outside the backdoor. Reaching down, he grabbed a bin-liner in each hand and heaved them away.

There were two types of movement allowed in the enclosure. You could walk straight into the centre and straight back out. This was okay from any direction. Otherwise you could circle the interior anti-clockwise. Nothing else made sense. Clasping the two bin-liners, he made straight for the centre and dropped them down. As the bottles moaned away, fifteen tongues emerged from the ditches, their flinty taste-buds winking in the sunlight.

He fetched an old metal bucket from the shed and filled it with water from the brook. Back in the enclosure he tore open the first bin liner and began preparing the bottles. First the labels had to go. They were whiskey mainly, some were vodka, some gin. Before his mother had fallen ill, his father had barely drunk. When he did it was just a glass or two. Whiskey usually, the quality stuff. None of this own-brand shite. Somehow it was soulless. Now he put away one or two a day. Had been for months. Lost his job, obviously. They'd given him compassionate leave at first, but he'd never gone back. Adam shook his head.

He piled up the labels and washed the bottles out as best he could. Most of them were okay, the odd one had a brain of fungus in the base; you had to scrape it out with a stick. One by one he skinned and cleaned them, stacked them out in a fragile arc around his legs. In the end there were forty-three. Thirty-eight whiskey, three vodka, two gin. As the sun began to set, he left the enclosure, slung the dregs back into the brook and went home to cook dinner for his father.

Darkness crept over the fens. Adam Oak, his black curls shivering in the breeze, closed the backdoor and headed towards the copse. On over the fence he scrabbled, across the brook and into the scattered trees. He collected firewood and built a massive pyre in the centre of his enclosure. Then he used the labels stripped from the bottles as kindling and sent the whole lot up. As the logs took, the light of the flame filled the enclosure like a ripple. The banks reflected most of it back inside, but where it broke through the causeways, the fifteen painted trails bolted off into the night. Outside the world danced with shadows and uncertainty. As Adam circled the fire, it cast his own shadow outwards like a compass point, dark and unsettled.

He picked up a bottle and patted it into his palm. He walked over to the first ditch. At the edge he stopped. The heat had vanished, his distance from the fire severing the cord of warmth. A chill passed through him as he lifted the bottle up to his lips and blew into the neck. It hummed a low reply. The signal. He tilted his head back to the stars, drew a deep breath and screamed from the pit of his stomach. The scream rang out around the copse and across the fields. A flock of sheep looked up startled, the ewes hurrying their lambs from the tree-line. No sooner had he released the scream than he'd raised the bottle high up above his head and pelted it down into the ditch. The bottle pulsed along its course and exploded into jagged teeth.

His heart pounded. That was the scream. That was the fucking scream! Right there for everyone and no-one to hear. It was the scream intended for his mother's face as she lay there pitiful and blameless. The scream for his father's face as he sat there shrivelling. The scream. His breathing was rapid. His throat was sore. This was real, and for the first time in months he savoured reality. Lost to the surge of adrenalin, he returned to the fireside and snatched another bottle; another moment. This time the scream felt even better. It hurt even more. His lungs, his throat, his head. They could all see where this was going. It was agony and it was good. A few more ditches and Adam could taste blood. He could taste it like he could taste the power of his enclosure. He hocked it up and spat it into each of the remaining bottles before committing them.

It took only ten minutes. Ten minutes of frenzy which seemed to pass with every atom of speed the universe could conjure. The glare of the fire, the heat. The chill as he arrived at the ditches. The release, the scream, the relief. And that sound, the sound of the glass shattering and the sheer ferocity with which he slammed it into each and every ditch but one. Ten minutes, and the enclosure was all that existed, bathed in flame. There was nothing else. No fear of the shadows beyond the perimeter, of a future which may or may not have lurked beyond the present. Just the immediacy of emotion, the taste of blood, the sound of screams. It all made so much sense here, controlled and contained.

And when it was over, and the bottoms of the ditches lay covered in blood-stained shards, he collapsed before the fire, still burning strong. As he peered into it he could no longer talk. His throat on fire, dissolved, every muscle in his body torn. His palms scorched. His head pounding. Dizzy and sick, he *had* been sick into the last few bottles, hadn't he? Hadn't he thrown up the two portions of beans on toast that he'd made not more than an hour before? Then, shortly afterwards, Adam Oak left the enclosure, *his* enclosure, for the final time. And his life, like the flames at its heart, danced away in front of his face.

3008AD. Archaeologists have excavated a small area of wasteland in the centre of an ancient English housing estate. They produced a preliminary report prior to full publication. The following is a short excerpt:

'The main feature to be uncovered during the recent investigations was an intriguing circular enclosure some ten metres in diameter, cut into the underlying chalk. The enclosure ditch was not continuous, but consisted of fifteen distinct segments designed to allow multiple routes of access via the intervening causeways. The original material from each ditch was piled up into an adjacent length of bank, no longer extant. The deliberate accessibility of the interior militates against the enclosure having served a defensive purpose. Rather, the accumulation of numerous shards of glass in the base of all but one of the ditches, and the discovery of a hearth at the enclosure's centre suggests a more social or ceremonial function. In particular, the glass has been attributed to BTA (bottle-type A) associated with the containment of high-strength alcoholic liquids. It is known that such liquids—freely available and known as 'spirits'—were commonly imbibed during the early third millennium AD as a form of social

ritual. On this evidence alone, it is likely that the enclosure formed the venue for a lively celebration or festival, encouraging widespread communal participation; a celebration of life. The gradual silting up, rather than deliberate backfilling, of the ditches suggests both that the festival was a one off event and that the site was subsequently intended to form a monument in lived memory. Analysis of residues from the glass suggests the spilling of blood, either through accidental injury or deliberate ritual, as well as the consumption of beans and wheat. The other major point of interest was the discovery of the remains of a sub-adult male (approx. 15 years) in crouched position adjacent to the central hearth. Cause of death is unknown, but the absence of a grave cut suggests either that he died where he fell, the victim of alcohol excess, or that he was offered up to the enclosure at the close of the ceremony. Either way, his peaceful repose gives no indication of trauma.'

Tibo

Naomi Grant

Oil on Board, 40.5 x 51.5 cm, 2007

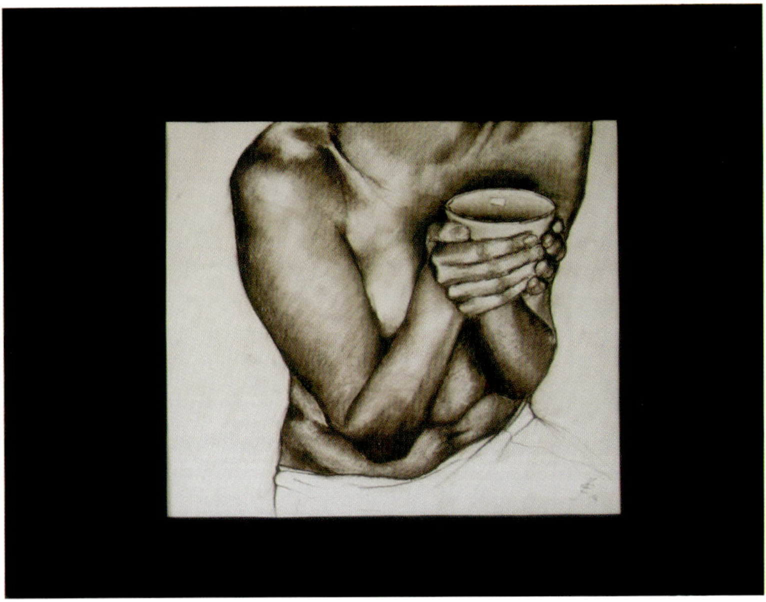

Hold

Simone Kotva

Mixed charcoal on cartridge paper, 38 x 36 cm, 2008

Lonesome Mustang

Cortland Rankin

Digital Photograph, 2007

Reds, Greens, & la Sacré-Coeur

Cortland Rankin

Digital Photograph, 2008

blueyellowjazz

Catherine Williams

Pencil on Paper, 10 x 15 cm, 2007

PC160890b

Ian Heames

Watercolor on Board, 21 x 28", 2007

Maria

Beatrice Priest

Oil on Canvas, 30 x 30 cm, 2007

Sarah

Beatrice Priest

Oil on Canvas, 76 x 50 cm, 2007

Kamuzu Stadium, Blantyre, Malawi, 2007

Owen Holland

Ilford XP2 b/w, 7 x 5", 2007

Sleeping Cat
Megan Davies
Watercolor & Ink, 4 x 4", 2007

Earth - Life - Peace

Hazel Lambert (Hazel Hancock)

Digital Photograph, 2007

China Shop

Eley Williams

'WOULD THE MINOTAUR MOO?' I watched the lampshade cough some fiery and tufted dust against the shadows of his bedroom.

'I imagine it would bellow rather than moo.'

I shut the book closed with a clap of covers. Bernard's face turned on the pillow at the sound, eyes still jammed together with sleepiness. 'So, it would speak?' he asked.

'I don't think Ovid mentioned either way. I *imagine* he bellowed. The minotaur, not Ovid. Or perhaps it would bell like a stag.'

His eyes began working fast under their fastened lids, rolling from one thought to another. He did a similar thing when playing chess. 'It wouldn't have anyone to talk too, anyway,' I added. I intended this in a fatherly, practical way.

'No. I suppose not.'

Bernard moved in the sheets, tossing maggoty-fat in his duvet.

My sleepy son. Pearl from my grit.

I am not sure I like Bernard.

I have tried all the things that fathers do in the adverts with their children. I ruffle his hair, I touch his shoulders. I sometimes pass him rugby balls. Neither of us play rugby; I bought one of the balls expressly so that I could pass it to him over the breakfast-table and excite the dogs.

The word 'prodigy' has often been bandied about concerning Bernard, banded about him. I'll rephrase that: 'banded' sounds too restrictive. Although certainly, as my wife reminds me, there is a restrictive pressure upon him to perform well with this buzzing bright blob of a brain in his head. 'Branded', perhaps. Does the term 'prodigy' give him both a plinth and a yoke? A yinth. A ploke. He is horribly clever, whatever. He is playing chess against a shiny—the shiniest—computer the day after tomorrow ('And him only twelve!'); if he wins, I will see this little pillow-propped head inked and doubled in all the newspapers the next morning. The pictures will have him holding a cheque larger than his whole body.

The headlines will have exclamation marks. He will be a national treasure, Bernard, my son.

'What's the describing-word for something by Ovid?'

'The adjective? And I thought you had no time for English!' I said, and poked him in the crease under his ribs, beneath the blankets, in the bed, in my house, where he used to be ticklish as a baby. He has never actually said such a thing. He was always a maths boy—the mathsiest boy—and I supposed there was no room in that mind to be interested in anything else. I had never thought to ask. Was he even taught English?

Nerd, geek, dweeb. They sound like brands of sweets. I work in advertising. Everything's A Brand!

Despite my nudgings he stayed inert and answered his own question with another, steadily. 'Ovine?'

'Ovidian, I think. Ovine means something to do with sheep.'

'And bovine to do with cows?'

'Yes. Cows that moo.'

The eyelids paused in their flickery; cogs of thought were now grinding deep in his head, deeper than the thin slip of skin over his eyeballs could betray to me.

I have learnt from twelve, gingerly curious years of Daddydom that an adult should never presume to understand what it is that his child is thinking. I cannot create thoughts like a child; I think in bullet points and animated .gifs and spreadsheets. I am not sure when the switch happened exactly, when the adult rushed in and threw the toys out of the cradle of my mind. But I do know that I just cannot see things like Bernard. This bedroom, for example: for a child it is caves and dens and monsters and oceans and lava. The only potential I can rustle up is the potential sound of a shower, the potential smoothing of linen.

So I cannot see like a child, cannot think like a child, cannot reason like a child, and certainly cannot see what my horribly clever son Bernard, whose very breath is calculation, might be thinking.

'Can you read it to me again tomorrow?' he asked.

'This is the third time I've read it to you this month.'

'I like it.'

'You like it.'

'Yes.'

The eyes opened, and looked at the ceiling. I watched him for a while, then turned off the bedside light.

I remained on the edge of the bed.

I realised I was using the slackness, then the tautness, then the falling slackness of the cover over his lungs to gauge whether he was still alive. Apparently his eyes were, resolutely, not going to shut any time soon; I could see a white crescent of gleam on their wet open surface in the moonlight.

When had I last held him? Did it matter?

I am tired.

'Good night, Bernie.'

I left.

◈◈◈

A husband and wife are in bed. They have been married for some time, and there is an unworn stripe of cold sheet separating them. I am facing the door, she the window. My tongue is playing with a boomerang of toothpaste that has lodged in the corner of my mouth.

And we're off.

She asked, 'Did he get to sleep alright?'

Exchanging words is a lot like holding hands.

'Yes,' I lied. 'I read the story then left. Theseus and the Minotaur again.'

'I read the minotaur one to him yesterday!'

'He obviously really likes it.'

She moved, and all the angles in the room changed. 'He asked me whether minotaurs could moo.'

'Minotaurs, plural? There is only one Minotaur.'

'Pedant.'

Exchanging words is nothing like holding hands. 'Marital' and 'martial' are very similar words, if the 'I' bothers to move around.

I said, 'He asked me the same thing. About the mooing.'

'I said it could speak. Like Ermintrude.'

'Ermintrude?'

'From the "Magic Roundabout".'

I thought, wife: you are banality itself. You are lumpen, waxen, dry-lipped, salty. I am strong and wayward. I might consider myself swarthy, if I only really understood what that word meant.

She continued: 'Why did you set him off on the Minotaur thing anyway? Why read that story to him? I think it startled him.'

'What.' I am too tired for question marks.

'He looked petrified when I was reading it.'

'No one talks about *mooing* if they're petrified.'

'It's a scary story. He's still only young and I just thought that the whole Ermintrude thing could bring some levity to the situation.'

'Ermintrude from the "Magic Roundabout" trapped in a labyrinth, feasting upon the ripe flesh of Athenian youth, is the very stuff of nightmares.'

'Well!'

'Well.'

'Well, I wouldn't have been *put* in that position if you hadn't brought up minotaurs in the first place. He just can't afford to have nightmares with the chess tournament coming up.'

'He's too old to be having stories read to him, full stop. Twelve years old? He should be shooting up monsters on a games console. Or working out whether he likes girls. Or happy-slapping the elderly.'

She kicked me under the sheets. Her feet were freezing, and for some reason I could tell her toenails were too long. This clothing-less, fleshy trapezium of a woman with nails on her feet is sleeping next to me. This is unbearable. I stopped nudging the toothpaste on the side of my mouth.

'I want you to take him to Crowley's farm to see the cows tomorrow.'

This warranted not only a question mark, but an actual turn of my actual head. 'What? Why?'

'To calm Bernard. Make him see they're not frightening.'

'What?'

'Cows. I don't want him developing a complex about them. He looked properly freaked out by the story you've been feeding him, by the cow element.'

'I don't—'

'All I'm asking, David, is that you just take him on a father-son trip into a field there; show him that they're not big and scary. Tomorrow.'

That is the second time this conversation that she has used the word 'scary'. Do not think I have not noticed. 'When have I ever, *ever*, taken Bernard on a father-son trip?'

'That may well be my exact point.'

◈◈◈

I started the engine, and enjoyed flexing my knuckles on the steering wheel. For no reason, of course; my hands need not be nimble at this point. They could be stiff, gouty, weak. But it looked good, the flexing. I did it again.

'Seatbelt on?' I asked as Bernard slid into the front passenger seat.

He fiddled. 'Yes.'

'Good.'

Ignition, and out of the driveway.

'Do you feel confident about it?' I murmured, a mile further on.

'About what?'

'The tournament tomorrow. Against the computer with the funny name.'

'Yes.'

'Great.'

He was all hunched against the window, marbling his cheek-flesh against it. He is quite a squashy kid.

There was something of a myth about bloodlines, I've always thought. A magic lie in the concept of descendancy that I found I had bought into, even when I realised Bernard was not going to be the hero-son every father wants. He was a fat-headed, tuggy-fisted mewling little personling, like every other baby in the ward. Always a squashy kid, like this.

But twelve years ago I thought something along the lines of, 'I am begetting! As I was myself begat! I will start a dynasty, a race of men, and they shall sing and laugh and talk of fire and of sun! And they shall be stronger than all other sons, and shall prove themselves as such in battle!'. Was that really what I had thought of fatherhood? Of sonhood? 'All shall look upon my son's works (mighty, many, manly) and despair!'. That is the thought which had first come to my mind, swelling, proud, ridiculous, when the nurse with the crackly plastic mask had wiped the gel off my wife's midriff in a white room and told me about unborn Bernard's gender.

Back in the car, Bernard and I both winced as we sped over a piece of pheasant road-kill lying rainbow-faced in the middle of the tarmac.

Sons. A myth that smelt of leather and soap and the outdoors. A tale of fishing trips, and bearhugs, and sagas; a son shall go on quests, shall still butterflies with their breath, wear dungarees and ride tricycles and span the land with a host of weapons and lovers and beards. They need not be good at things like chess.

Look at you, you clever, weak sapling. You seedling, busy about the head with bees.

'You missed the turning, Dad.'

I am having an affair, Bernard.

No. I cannot just tell you.

'Righto,' I said.

Why did we call you 'Bernard', I wondered as the car looped back around the roundabout the way it had come. You are growing into a squashy, pale librarian of a Bernard-man. I can envisage you, Bernard, getting older over your chess set the way I have over my desk, the way your mother has over her dressing-table. Maybe you will run to fat, and cold thick wrists will worm out of your cuffs, collared with a gold watch with a gold face, and you will wear two too shiny brown shoes, and you will have yellow teeth with black edges. You will have sweet-smelling hair. Brilliant-Bernard the Young will turn into a pawn-pushing St. Bernard, the too-big dog with jowls and a barrel around his neck.

Boys should like dinosaurs or jet fighters, not the Minotaur. My son should like dinosaurs or jet fighters. Bernard did not *like* chess, I am pretty sure of that at least. He just did it, without thinking.

He was so clever with it, of course. The cleverest son a man could hope for, cleverer than his old Dad who missed the turning. If you took both our heads and filled them with ball-bearings, his might even hold more ball-bearings than mine.

He thinks of bishops as oblique, knights as horse-headed, queens as tall and kings as crucial, stunted. He is very careful to call the castles 'rooks'. They are not named after the birds, I once told him when we last played a match; they're named after the Persian word for 'chariot'. Rook-birds enjoy carrion, chariot-rooks enjoy charging. He nodded, then took my queen. He was five years old.

The less said about 'pawns' back in my schooldays, the better. Pawns from a pawn-shop. Pawn from the top shelf. Haha. Bernard did not go to school but was instead tutored by his mother, my wife, at home. She was also his manager, and had arranged all the press conferences for after Wednesday's tournament. Bernard had been managed since the manger.

I think my wife knows Bernard quite well.

I know some facts about Bernard, however; vital statistics that I have observed in his natural habitat. I recall he has developed a curious hatred of draughts. Or was it chequers. Whichever, I also know he loved the names of the different chess-gambits: Benko, Albin, Elephant. And I knew of the movements of his eyelids during matches, and of the way he folded his hands in his lap between moves, holding them clasped inward like two crabs pressing their bellies together. There was no victory possible for any opposition once he did that.

The farm was advertised on a post, and I flapped the indicator on.

I do not understand chess, so I do not play it with him any more. Or, more precisely, I do not understand how Bernard plays chess. He plays it both mathematically and naturally, pushing pieces into brackets in his head. He mouths when he makes moves and his fingers twitch. With his head kept quite still, glutted on numbers, his fingers and eyelids snap involuntarily at invisible abacus-strings. Pink, soft, wandering fingers

There is no air of glory about him, either, when he wins. I am an air-punching man, a hooting man; HELL YEAH. But Bernard just nods at the job well done, then leaves the hall. His competitions are always held in halls; I think my wife arranges it this way so that the vaulted décor emphasises how small he is. The trainers I bought him trot squeakily on glazed parquet flooring after every match.

I wish I could say that he is a mathematician and that I am a wordsmith, and that he is just a different chip off the old, bigger block. But that just is not true: my thoughts sag and bow inward, unlike his, which work with gears and steam.

As for my achievements, the bacon I have brought home? My greatest triumph, the reason that I am pointed out with hors d'oeuvre-laden fingers and greasy lip-clacking congratulations at my wife's dinner parties; the greatest feat that might ever bring that smiley silverfox presenter out from behind a bush to whisk me away to a studio on This Is Your Life; the jotting in the 'Whatever Became of…' column left blank thus far in my school yearbook next to a picture of my head: my greatest conquest lay in advertising, conceived at a board-meeting. Everyone loved me for a week. I am the man that decided to have 'I Got Rhythm' as the background music for a new brand of prune-juice. Clients touched my shoulders. I punched the air, at the time. I hooted.

So in sum, Bernard, you are better than your father.

Can you imagine giving birth to a baby with the head of a bull?

At least I do not put undue pressure on you, unlike your mother, Bernard. It is not because I do not care, but because I care so much that I do not want to help you.

That is because I resent you, Bernard.

I can never tell you that, either.

'Where are we going again?' Bernard asked, not complaining.

'To the Crowley's farm to look at cows.'

The car gnawed into a gravelled stop by the swing-gate. We pulled in, and I registered the cows in the field beyond. 'I know *that*,' Bernard said. 'Why are we going to the Crowley's farm to look at cows?'

'For your mother.'

He considered. 'Will there be a bull?'

'I imagine so.'

He turned back to the window and then, quietly, opened the car door.

◈◈◈

I swung open the field's gate for him, then closed it behind us.

'Right,' I said. The cold spring air embroidered my breath in front of me. 'There are your cows.'

He stood for a minute. We watched them.

'Milk,' I said. 'Milk, beef, gravy, satchels. Cud. All kinds of things come from those animals.'

He shifted on his feet.

'Lovely day for it!' I said, and spread my hands wide. This was not entirely a lie. There were, certainly, many details I disliked about the scene. The crispy rinds of earth blistered up into cowpats around my feet, for example. The cows' blue tongues and swagging blue saliva; the way one of the cows is ginghamed unevenly in the light through the chicken-wire. There are brambles over there that could catch on our clothes, on mine and Bernard's skin; springtime brambles that are thickening up for their blackberries. I hate blackberries almost as much as I hate prunes. Trussed up, bulbous, suppurating excuses for blackcurrants, that is all blackberries are. There is a wood beyond the cows that is full of cherry blossom.

'Did you say something, Bernard?'

'No.'

I was more accustomed to the indoors than out here; I could feel the cold in unexpected folds of my face. In my face's inboxes. I could feel the plaque on my teeth. Bernard looked a little cold too with raw red and pink patches competing on his face and hands, so I pulled him closer to my jacket. We squinted at the nearest cow.

'How do you feel, looking at them? Feel calmer? See at that one? The yellowy one that looks like that politician with the eyebrows? I like her. Watch them stand up, sit down, mill about. It's therapeutic, don't you think, Bernard? Like watching goldfish in a barrel.'

'You shoot goldfish in a barrel.'

'What's that?'

'It's fish in a tank that are supposed to be relaxing. To watch. You're thinking of "like shooting fish in a barrel".'

'Barrel of a gun. Gun on a tank. Armoured tanks.'

'That's an entirely different kettle of fish.'

'Good one,' I say.

'The word "bull-dozer" is a funny thing, isn't it, Dad?'

'Yes.'

I was aware of all the details in the field. I could stand and count the eyelashes on the cows, the blades of the grass, the number of flies. Even the bluebottles' bodies have a lustre in this light. The cherry blossom in the distance is pink in a brown wood. Chocolate and quartz. The textures of the field hurt my eyes.

'You feel more relaxed, hmm?' I said, looking down at him.

'I like them.'

'You have to do well on Wednesday, Bernard.'

'Mum always wants me to do well.'

'Yes. Don't you, too?'

'I guess.'

'Well, that's good.'

'I'm a special boy,' said Bernard, clearly quoting his mother. He was looking sadly at one of the cows trying to scratch its nose with a hindhoof.

'Yes. Yes you are.'

'So was the Minotaur. And look what happened to him.'

'His father put him in a labyrinth,' I said, and thought about lunging in for a jokey head-ruffle.

'His dad was a bull,' Bernard corrected me. 'His mother's husband put him in a labyrinth.'

'That is true.'

'Bulls eat grass,' he added after a while, disappointed.

'That is also true.'

'He ate meat in the book. He eats meat in the book.'

'He certainly devoured people. Maybe he oughtn't have, however. If he'd just stuck to grazing, maybe it would have been fine. Digestively speaking.'

'I doubt there was grass in the labyrinth.'

'Me too.'

Is this bonding with Bernard? Trying to work out what his head is doing, where it is going? Could I tell you anything now, Bernard? That I am afraid your mother and I are having problems. That I am going to go to my secretary's house after this, and that her house is way out of town. That my secretary is an American and says 'milk' in the most charming way, that she is supple and plush when all else is brittle. I think you would like her. She eats croissants really very delicately.

You are a strange, cloying little boy and I have let you down.

'Do you think the Minotaur spoke to the people they sent to be eaten by him?' Bernard asked. He was swivelling a finger in his ear.

'I thought we decided he couldn't speak at all.'

'He must have been lonely.'

'That cow has ticks on it. Let's look at this one instead.'

'The trick with chess,' Bernard said, suddenly looking at the cow I pointed out, 'is knowing a move ahead.'

There is a black cow in a big red triangle on the side of the road, on a sign behind us.

'So I've heard.'

'Not a single move ahead, Dad. Not really even two moves ahead. It's something to do with knowing, when the other person sits down opposite you, what their first move will be.'

'I don't know how to do that, Bernard.'

You do not hug a calculator, I told myself.

'We could let the cows out of the field,' I then said, looking at the wood beyond. 'That's not supposed to happen.'

My son said something, but I could not catch the words.

'We could leave the gate open for them,' I said.

'Open the gate?'

'If we wanted.'

'We could follow them.'

'If we wanted.'

Bernard took his finger out of his ear. 'Would the cows be alright?'

'I don't know.'

'You don't know,' Bernard said, and he hugged me.

I touched his shoulders, and we watched the cows.

The Invention of Dice

Benjamin Morris

THE RABBIT IS THE FIRST to notice her. When the woman walks into the living room of my house, palming a jet-black, pearl-handled Luger, we are so lost in our game of Scrabble that it takes the apoplectic hisses and grunts of the creature in the corner to get any of us to raise our heads.

"What, fatty?" Evelyn scowls at the cage. We have never named the beast; it never felt necessary.

"Oh," she says, seeing. "Hell—hello."

The woman with the pistol—tall, slim as a river iris, in a saffron yellow dress and pumps—appears above us, drumming her fingertips rhythmically across the barrel. In the sudden stillness of the room it sounds like raindrops pattering on the skylight.

"Yes?" she asks coolly. She is now close enough to see that I am losing badly. "Have you forgotten something?"

"Wh—what?" stammers Amanda. Her silvery-blond hair shivers, collapses over her face. Thom twiddles a *d*; two measly points.

"You've misspelled *assonance*. It has one *s*."

"No it doesn't—I mean, we checked the—are you going to—with that—"

"Don't tempt me," the woman says, cocks the pistol, and fires a round square into the center of the board.

◈◈◈

The neighborhood in which I live, like many others in Edgerton, is rarely prone to acts of violence or extremity in any form. We have storms, occasionally, in which we lose a few loblolly pines, but the bastards usually have it coming anyway. The most sensational events of late were when Marcia Keller's son backed over his own cat in the driveway (nicked it, really, no blood that we could see), or when widower Spinks uprooted three of his prize-winning dogwoods slain by the early frost. To be honest, we don't even speak to each other much, except to borrow the odd chainsaw or Dirt Devil, and we like this state of affairs just fine. The chatty, eager newcomers to the area are inevitably ground down by our smiling lethargy, and over time either decamp for subdivisions which actually have names, or better yet, just stop trying. Few of the folks around here even conceive of their neighborhood as a place to live in so much as a waystation to pass through, a terminal from which one connects to the Piggly Wiggly, the beauty parlor, the mall. For most of us, it simply doesn't exist.

This is the real reason I am so rankled at what has just happened. Not only is this woman's intrusion unsettling and terrifying and life-threatening and the like, but its grammar belongs to a language of behavior that we have never seen. It is positively *rude.*

◈◈◈

The rabbit hisses again, and the woman, whose name is Camellia Martin, pops off another round in the general direction of the cage to shut it up. We don't know how many rounds she has left; after she sat the four of us down on the center couch in a neat little petrified row, she walked around the room for a while shooting numerous holes in the floor—I can't tell if she sees other, smaller rabbits in the house that the rest of us have never noticed before, but I'm not sure I want to ask. One thing is for sure: that pert white handbag of hers holds more than one clip.

That said, it occurs to me in a small moment of pride that I live in a house that is remarkably well insulated—not only does it muffle my energy bills, but it takes care of the sound of gunshots pretty good too. But despite my pride I don't expect any neighbors to be knocking on our door anytime soon to check on all the fuss (not like they would anyway)—so we're running low on options for the time being. Nor do we know why Camellia is here, exactly, or what she intends to do; leaving our various offices yesterday, this is the last thing that any of us would have expected. It feels as though the evening had been composed simply of random letters on a board—artichoke dip, pizza, beer, the perfect Labor Day weekend—until someone put down a tile in just the right place, and magically a word appeared.

"So, are you going to shoot us?" Thom ventures at length, crossing and uncrossing his arms. Thom is a broker, and he would want to put in a call first.

"Hm?" Camellia has laid the pistol down on my mother's secretary and has begun rifling through its drawers.

"Well, it's been two hours already, and you've shot pretty much everything else in the room, and I was just wondering..."

"Don't be silly."

"So you're not going to shoot us." Already Thom is running futures in his mind.

"Now why would I want to do that? You are sitting on a beautiful Greek Revival and the blood would be a mess. It would take months to get it out, and do you know who does that kind of work anymore?"

"No'm."

"Neither do I. Now be *still*, for the love of God."

"But I need to stretch," protests Amanda.

"Fine. Stretch. Just get it over with."

Amanda stands, unfurls her fingers and toes, starts to yawn but quickly claps a hand over her mouth. "Sorry," she peeps.

"This is ridiculous," Evelyn says, and goes to pour herself a Coca-Cola.

As she pads out of the room I glance over at the rabbit, which has finally quieted down. Fat, surly, and dust-colored, it has survived its brief existence as the main attraction in a shooting range reasonably well, its shavings mostly scattered to the floor and the sweet acrid tang of gunsmoke wafting through the holes in the wall around it—though for some reason it keeps trying to grab ahold of its ear with its left paw, needing, I reckon, like the rest of us, something to sit there and fidget with before the true madness begins to set in. On closer inspection—Camellia is still occupied with Mom's desk—I lean over and see that one of the bullets fairly exploded its water bottle, and now the beast is utterly soaked. All the commotion has furthermore caused its incontinence to kick up, and with all the scrambling around its cage and dodging bullets and whatnot it is now fully garnished with its own urine. I don't know how much my partners-in-innocence here on the couch have dealt with wet rabbit in the past, but I can say this much: given enough time, piss, and panic, that critter there in the corner is going to smell absolutely *foul*.

Evelyn returns, ice clinking faintly ahead of her. Judging by the warmth dawning over her face, there's more than just Coke in that glass. She folds one leg underneath her as she settles herself on the couch, retrieves her knitting from the end table and sets back to work on her sock. I have always admired the way Evelyn, a movie critic at the paper, can find the most comfortable spot in a room—instinctively gravitating to the softest surface, the quietest nook, the space in which her body is freed from edges or corners and can focus simply on the task at hand.

Amanda begins to shift.

"What is it, sweetheart?" I ask, cradling her shoulder. We have been seeing each other for just a few weeks, since she hustled me down at the pool hall, and we are still testing out our names for one another: thus far she has mostly been *sugar* and *darling*, and I have done time as *honeybunch*, *sweetpea*, and my absolute favorite, *lazy-daisy*.

"I want a drink *too*," she sniffs.

"I know you do, honey. Me too. Gin or vodka?"

"Gin. No, vodka. No. Something what tastes like a peach."

Camellia looks up, holding her gaze like a shiv. "A Martini," she orders. "Dry. And bring me that phone by the fridge."

"Yes, ma'am. Thom? Can't carry everything myself." While we're at it, I reckon we might as well bring in the whole tea service—smoked salmon and butter crackers, maybe some of that good crab dip my pastor sometimes brings over.

Thom waits for Camellia's assent, given by a flick of her wrist in the direction of the kitchen. Silently we leave the living room, only to gasp for conversation as soon as we are out of range. We make a fine pair: I have no idea who this woman is, what she is doing in my house, or what she wants from us. I only know that she is taking an interest something powerful in my mother's desk, which I have barely touched since my dad died. Thom, on the other hand, has no idea how to make a martini, and now that we are alone his hands have begun trembling too violently anyway to do anything except place a silver shaker into them and save myself the trouble.

Setting out a glass, I grab the bottle from above the fridge and drop a pony of Beefeater over the ice. "Do you think we can talk things out with her," Thom asks, "or do you think she responds to reason like she responds to Scrabble?"

"I think we need to find out what she's here for, and if we can, give it to her. Or help her find it. Or something. Anything to get her out. I'm worried she might go crazy, and then we're all screwed."

"Especially the rabbit," he adds.

I snort.

"But she seems to know what she's doing here," he continues, fishing an olive out of the jar. "If you look at the way she came in and took charge, it's like she thinks she belongs. She knows where everything is."

This is an insightful point, rare for Thom: when my father and I moved to this house years ago, he had lost his job in insurance and we were looking to find something more modest for the two of us—a buyer had come along at just the right time for our old place, and Pop wanted a fresh start in a new neighborhood. Nor can I blame him for trying to make a clean breast of it—but he did move all our old furniture into the place, including everything that belonged to my mother: her bed, her Queen Anne, the ottoman on which Evelyn's feet now perch. But I only know of all this through him, as I never knew my mother: she died ushering me into the world. And now that he's gone and followed her, I'm left with the beds, the couches, and the beechwood secretary to which Camellia has gravitated.

Nor have I ever met any of Mom's family; almost the day after her funeral, as I lay gurgling in the hospital nursery, my father broke off contact with them as easily as if he had snapped a piece of celery, and I have only the faintest notion of who they are and where they live. Which is why Thom's point is so intriguing. She looks nothing like me or my mother, but am I related to this pistol-toting, rabbit-terrorizing banshee?

◈◈◈

We've taken long enough; we don't want to seem suspicious. Thom and I have not decided anything; for now, we have agreed to watch our pieces on the board as it develops, and if we are not too spooked by the sight of that pistol (which looks as lovingly maintained as the nails on the hand that holds it) then we may try to engage Miss Camellia in some further conversation.

But this was only *our* idea. When we return, drinks in hand, Camellia is now standing, absorbed in a slim piece of paper the color of butterscotch—my mother's writing paper, which I'd recognize a mile away for all the times I've seen my father holding it, folding it and refolding it, lost in the act of tracing over and over again the trail of her own elegant hand. Nights like that, when he took to rereading her letters on the couch, I'd have to fetch a comforter from the hall closet for him, make sure he kept warm—knowing I'd find him in the same spot the next morning, having forgotten about his bed. In Dad's last year I'm not sure he slept in his own room once.

Settling back down next to Amanda, who nearly weeps at the sight of her Fuzzy Navel, I cross my legs and engage in a little private consultation with Dr Jack Daniels. Across the room, Thom places Camellia's drink down on the sleeve of an envelope, and sets the telephone on the desk. The gun is within his reach, if he would just shove Camellia out of the way and lunge for it—but for some reason, either his fear or his manners, or the fact that he wouldn't know which end is for business and which is for pleasure, Thom backs off step by step in reverse until his knees graze the couch and nearly grow mouths of their own to sing out in joy.

We are back where we started, four peas in a pickle: Thom has proved his uselessness once again, Evelyn, tired of knitting, has taken to reading the Scrabble dictionary, and after just half a drink Amanda has that dreamy look creeping over her which I am pretty sure means she wouldn't mind putting on some belly-rubbing music. Though we are again fresh out of options—belly-rubbing is probably the next-to-last thing we could try at this point, beaten only by asking the crazy woman politely to leave—I was right about one thing, at least: the scent of a rabbit which is both pissed-off and pissed-on has begun to waft its way across the room, leaving a tang on the tongue that nigh ruins my chat with the good doctor.

"What *is* that horrible smell?" Camellia sets the letter down on the desk. So it *has* made it that far.

"What, the peach?"

"I think it's coming from the rabbit, ma'am," offers Thom, and crawls back behind his glass.

"Christ! It reeks. Do something about it, *now*—can't you see I'm trying to work?"

Casting around for a moment and coming up empty—a potted fiscus wouldn't do much good, nor a newly cratered Scrabble board—Thom grabs Amanda's drink out of her hand and throws whatever's left into the cage. Wonderful—now the beast smells like piss, hate, and peaches. *Gnaaah*, it hisses, pumping its back legs wildly, kicking the predator it can't see.

"You bastard!" Amanda shrieks. "I was drinking that!"

"Yes, but she said—"

"You goddam sonofa—"

"Honey, sweetheart," I try. "Baby—"

"You shut up too!" She slaps me on the arm, *hard*, and in the silence that follows I hear belly-rubbing drop to rock bottom on the list.

"Oh, shut up, all of you," Evelyn tosses off. "Just shut—up."

"Listen to your friend," Camellia warns, picking up the pistol, cracking the chamber and checking the clip. She holds her tone in the same hand: "I'm nearly done here, so don't make me stay longer than I planned."

"Yes'm," we all chime, and rearrange ourselves on the couch, furious at one another but relieved to have reset our situation, to have reshuffled the deck. The rabbit, on the other hand, seems to have hit some kind of wall: amid its snarls and kicks, it has now begun to hurl itself against the side of the cage. In the two years the beast moved in, I've never known it to behave like this—and granted, while the stress of the last few hours has been considerable, none of *us* have reached our breaking points yet. For a second it seemed Amanda was about to, but either her aim was off (was she going for my face?), or—contrary to what I thought of her, and what first drew me to her the night she dogged me out of that fifty—she simply doesn't have it in her. Or did she miss deliberately? At this thought disappointment steals into my heart, the kind that can't be chased away by another shot of schnapps. But the rabbit, having lost whatever composure a rabbit can be said to possess, now seems to feel nothing but rage—sweet, frothing, limpid rage enough to make a man wonder at the sight.

"Miss Camellia?" I venture.

"What."

"I don't mean to interrupt you"—this is not entirely true—"but I'm worried about this little guy over here. He doesn't seem to be doing too well."

"And that's my problem?" She cocks her left eyebrow, aims it right at me.

"No ma'am—no, it's not. Not yours specifically. It's more like all our problem. It's distracting us, and that's causing us to distract you, and I was just wondering if we could just let it out, take it away somewhere. Then you could do whatever you have to do in peace. And we wouldn't bother you."

"Wouldn't bother you no more," Amanda chirps.

"That's right," echoes Thom.

"Sure." Evelyn has never been a team player.

After a moment's thought Camellia sighs, emitting a small billowy cloud of mingled distaste and resignation that this is, unfortunately, an excellent idea. This rabbit, now defecating frantically in its little hotbox of a cage, has become a living nightmare, emitting an unbearable stench and a low, variable squitter of noises known to no living animal. Nor is Camellia an unreasonable woman, I think, just someone who has a clear vision of the future ahead of her and who is unwilling to allow chance elements or deviations to enter into that vision. She is beautiful, if severe, and she could be a little more gun-shy for my taste, but as far as hostage-takers go, we could do worse. Suddenly I find myself feeling deeply sympathetic towards Camellia Martin: like us, *she* never wanted any of this to happen, and *of course* she'll do what she can to lighten the burden of the situation. What does it matter if it's of her own making? As my dad used to say, it's in gravy and gunfire that the subtleties get lost.

"Fine," she says at length. "Do whatever you have to do. Just be quick about it." See, I want to say, she's not so bad.

"Yes ma'am." I turn to Thom. "Can you give me a hand?"

He shrugs, and we stand and appraise the situation. Wanting no part in this, the girls shift to the far side of the couch, Amanda taking Thom's drink with her. "What do you think," he says, rolling up his crisp white sleeves, "about just taking the cage wholesale? That way we can put it outside or in the garage."

"Outside," I say. "We can use the porch door from the kitchen."

"But what if we spill its, you know..."

"Can we just go?"

The rabbit snorts, retches, hopping in place as we approach. The way forward, I see, will not be easy: not only is the cage oversized and unwieldy, but the shots that Camellia took at it earlier—the reasons for which I am just beginning to glimpse—have left its metal banding shorn and razor-sharp where it was grazed. Taking care to avoid grasping any edges on the outside, as well as to keep our fingers well out of reach of the foaming jaws on the inside, Thom and I position ourselves on either side of the cage and lift it up in one smooth motion.

Looking back on it now, it's difficult to remember what exactly happened first: the screams of Evelyn and Amanda as they recoiled in panic onto the couch, the torrents of profanity from Thom and myself joining to become a river, a flood of foul and unforgettable language, as the cage comes free in our hands, or the thunderclap that put a shrieking, deafening halt to everything in the room, including the rabbit, which lay quivering in a puddle of piss and blood at Camellia's feet.

Or maybe it has happened all at once, and suddenly we can barely breathe, the stillness in the room choking us, roaring in our ears and drowning us. Evelyn and Amanda are clinging to one another the way leaves cling to a tree in autumn, and Thom and I are frozen, fists like vice grips, to the cage. It takes a second shot and the final knotted jerk of the carcass on the floor to shake us out of our stunned silence: Camellia Martin, breathing heavily and spattered with blood across her shins and feet, nudges the corpse with her toe.

"It bit me," she says, simply. "It ran straight at me and it bit me," she repeats. A thin crimson crescent has formed on her ankle, loses shape, slides down beneath her heel and mingles with the blood pooling on the wooden floor. For an instant she has lost her composure, gaze locked on the mottled grey fur. "Why would it do that?" she asks, letting the gun dangle down onto one finger, smoke from the barrel spiraling gently into the air.

With death having entered the room, Thom is finally able to relax: "Because it knew this would happen," he says. "Animals can sense these things."

"That's nonsense," sputters Evelyn through the thick sobs and hair crowding her mouth. "That's just fucking nonsense and you know it!"

"What *do* I know?" Thom asks again, more serene than I have ever seen him. He turns to Amanda, who has still not uncurled from her fetal position on the couch, and places a hand on her knee. "Don't worry. Nothing bad is going to happen now." He lets go of the cage, the twin clasps anchoring it in place dangling mute and loose from where the rabbit had jarred them free, and gingerly I follow suit. "Really. I promise. Everything is going to be just fine. Isn't that right, Miss Martin?"

The woman still hasn't moved since noticing the bite on her ankle. She'll live; I've seen paper cuts deeper than that.

"Isn't that right?"

"That's right," Camellia returns, finally, regaining some sense of herself. "Yes, that's right." She is still alive, she remembers, she still has the gun, but there is a wire in her voice which we have not heard before. It is almost as if the slightest tremor would take hold and grow, would escalate until it set the whole edifice to collapsing.

"And it's time to go, isn't it." Thom continues, pressing the point. By now blood from the rabbit's corpse has crawled along the floor and is lining its little paths, the slim alleys and catchways along its tongue-and-groove joints, falling every now and then into one of the crevices her earlier shots created.

"Yes, it's time to go." At this point if the breeze blows too hard she might fall over.

"You have what you came for," he concludes, rearranging the pieces on the board: I am startled to see Thom walk directly over to Camellia and remove the gun from her hand, that long, lovely hand which is ever so slightly beginning to shake. He picks up the letter she had been holding and looks over at me. I shrug. He folds it in two and places it in her purse, places the purse in her hand, and takes her by the arm, marching her gently out of the room. As he passes me he hands me the Luger, which is the most solid and polished stone I have ever held in my life, and mouths, *nine-one-one.*

◈◈◈

It is not until some months after the incident, after all the cameras, the counseling and therapy, after Thom and Evelyn have eloped to Savannah, and long after Amanda and I have drifted into separate pool halls, that I get a call from my father's attorney. He is terribly apologetic—he lives in one of the older neighborhoods in town, where no one telephones after eight o'clock—saying there's nothing he can do, that despite the investigation, despite her arrest, the house, and most everything inside it, has reverted in title to my mother's half-sister. He doesn't say why, just that there's been a new reading of my mother's will, but I suspect that that slim piece of paper that left the house had something to do with it. He is a good lawyer, there will be a settlement, and honestly, I don't much mind—as my father used to say, I've never been known to fuss. But I do wonder if this new reading of Mom's will inquired after the smear of blood on that envelope, or whether the whisper of such a detail was lost in the roar of fortune flowing into the room, the river of smoke flowing out. I would not be surprised. It is often how these things work.

I am a terrific loser when it comes to board games; I can never see how the pieces are going to play out, or that many of these small wooden blocks have relationships to one another independent of how I happen to feel about them. They slide, or they flip, or they change colors when they click into place, or sometimes, inexplicably, they come to rest miles away from where they started. And these are just the pieces on the board, to say nothing of what happens inside the people moving them around. Then you throw in the invention of dice, and I can't help but wonder—*who came up with this torture?* Who was it centuries ago, garrisoned on a wall in the far north of anywhere, decided to choose their life's path by which number carved into a knob of bone happened to face the sky? *Six says we invade, ten says we don't.*

But regardless of what those numbers said, the idea caught on, and somebody marched into somewhere, and all these tricks and tokens and games were left clattering and mute in the streets as the boots ran rushing by them.

Writing with Light

Francesca Whitlum-Cooper

"EMILIE." The three short sounds trip off his tongue to be hidden under his breath. His hands pull down on his cheeks: she can hear the stubble rasp against his palms. He rocks forward in the chair to the creak of wood and denim. His breath is deliberate. Each suck of air is audible, pushing his jumper out from his ribs.

There is nothing else. There is only this. The sky might be blue, the park might be green, but she can pick out the individual fibres of his coat. She knows there's noise, there must be noise, but her ears are drowning in silence. It rings around her neck and in between her fingers.

She realises her mouth is wet, an abyss slowly filling. She almost gags on the swallow. In the place where she should feel her stomach there is an empty hole; a ball of blank; a sphere slowly swelling. The band of her jeans cuts like a knife. A hair dangles loose by her ear. Something—the wind—makes her sight wet. While she can see his pounding through his jumper, her heart seems to have stopped beating. Everything is concave behind brittle rib bones.

◈◈◈

For the photographer, life is a series of untaken photographs. Life is the one you don't develop as the fixer itches your fingers. Life is the moment you can't imagine. Stalling at the traffic lights as your eyes brim over; being left in a playground by your lover; leaving that lover in a deckchair as you storm to the carpark, a child under each arm. Life is running back home so fast that your heart beats bile at the back of your throat. Life is the mantra *I love my husband, I love my husband, I love my husband*. Life is being a terrible mother for serving fishfingers in front of the TV with hands that can't stop shaking. Life is being a terrible mother for ending an affair while your kids are on the swings.

Emilie is hiding in the bathroom where it began. Her back sinks against the icy tiles. The whiteness burns her eyes. This is the only room in the house without photos, without evidence, without the indelible stamp of "Emilie and Toby Rylance, loving couple, happy parents", unless you count the matching toothbrushes. Children's theme tunes waft up the stairs towards her. The kids are laughing, the smell of burnt baked beans is dissipating, but with it her resolve. She presses a monogrammed towel, a gift from a mother-in-law who appreciates monograms, into her mouth to hide the sobs that are gripping her body.

If she screws her eyes tight enough, she is back in a time when she and Toby were so happy it hurt. A constant ache from the smile on her face and eyes that saw nothing but him. Toby. Chirpy, charming, a ruffle of sandy hair and the best of intentions. Not one for grand gestures, but he'd always hold the door open for you and make tea while you collapsed on the sofa. It had been a long time, but it had always been for the long term. Even those first long weekends entwined in bed had had the explicit promise of a Future with a capital F. And she'd wanted it. She still wants it, but time has deadened, dulled that first blaze. Dating, wedding, babies: somewhere along the line myopic vision has opened out. When you're up at three in the morning for the third night in a row, little annoyances spark in the darkness.

Babies changed them. She loves them, but she's a bit fatter now, wider now, probably a bit more saggy now. Preparing lunchboxes and dressing two children under seven, there's no time to stare longingly into someone's eyes over breakfast. There's no time to kiss, to talk, to mention that your self-esteem is crawling along the skirting board and you don't think you can cope. The years of puke, wail and poo run into bedtime stories, ballet classes, the million and one things that stop you from talking about the one thing you want to say. She's seen it in Toby's face, seen the lines set in around his eyes, the constant state of being late. Kisses on lips recede into kisses on cheeks. Love is falling into bed and having time to say goodnight before sleep overwhelms you. They were tired and love was tired, and Richard just—

Richard. She doesn't know whether to scream or weep. She feels so stupid, so unbelievably, unutterably stupid. She can't see, she can't think: she can smell him on her jumper and guilt keeps smacking her in the stomach. There has always been guilt, but it's different now. Before, guilt was placated by a kiss, a touch, by the fact of having someone to hold you on rainy Thursday afternoons. Now there is nothing to disguise the ugliness, the deceit, the repulsive barrage of lies. She'd tricked herself into believing it had meant something: she'd known him, she'd trusted him, she'd thought it had meant something. How could it not mean something when so much was at stake? The drunken night of their housewarming, through eyes swimming in wine, it had been obvious. It had been natural to flirt, to tease, to be shocked when he followed her into the bathroom and pressed her up against the wall. Shocked, but thrilled: it was thrilling to be called beautiful, to be sexy, to have someone kiss your neck and not your forehead. Shit, the idea that someone could find you attractive when it'd taken you fifteen minutes to zip your dress up.

She can remember it all so clearly, more clearly now than through the alcoholic cloud at the time. Months seem less than minutes ago. Stumbling down the stairs in absolute terror, repeating all the time that it was only a kiss, only a kiss, only a kiss. She'd found Toby manning the barbecue and not let go of him all night, more affection in that one evening than in the year that preceded it. Richard's eyes had burned into her, laughing at the childishness that needed to be draped around her husband to undo what she'd just done. He'd gone back to Magda, little blonde Magda who'd squeezed herself specially into a pink silky thing, all the time desperate to be noticed by her husband. Magda had laughed, told jokes, played the fool, all for him. She was performing for an audience of twenty, but it was all for him. Emilie could see it, could see her desperate for him just to notice her. It was sickening, awkward. The conversation jarred: Magda's laugh was a little too shrill, a little too high, far too desperate, far too jaw-wobbling. Emilie hated him for not deigning even to smile at his desperate little wife: she wanted even more for the smile to come to her.

She'd gone to his house later in the week. Some stupid premise, a jumper they'd left behind, Magda's borrowed corkscrew. He'd watched her squirm. For all her attempts to be cool, aloof, she sat at the kitchen counter wringing her hands and blushing.

"Richard, about what happened, I..."

"You?" He's so nonchalant, leaning back, one eyebrow raised, daring her to keep going. His eyes are so dark she can hardly read them.

"I..." A stammer, a shiver, a deep inhalation. "I think we should just forget about it."

"You're beautiful."

The colour rushes to her cheeks, to her neck, her heart is exploding. "You can't say that, it's not fair, I—"

"Why?"

And she'd never answered that question, never spoken the words out loud. *Because it makes me want you; because it says you want me too; because we can't do this and things like that melt my resolve in an instant.* It had melted, and she'd melted, and he'd kissed her, and it was an inversion of everything that was right, an inversion of everything she believed in, but it had happened. *I love my husband, I love my husband, I love my husband.* That first thigh-shaking mantra from that first thigh-shaking afternoon, stumbling out of someone else's bed with stained lips and sick in her stomach. She couldn't stop shaking, she couldn't undo it. It was over, but it hung about them like stale smoke, a permanent gut-numbing blow.

"We have just had sex in your wife's bed, two feet away from your wedding photo."

"And yours."

"What?"

"On the dresser. Magda has a copy of your group wedding photo on the dresser, a photo of all of us back in the day."

"Oh my God."

And there it had been, her radiant face beaming back at her: white dress, silver-suited husband, blissfully happy. Magda on her left was already pregnant with Ralph, clinging to a more-thickly haired Richard. And Toby looking so unbearably happy that she wanted to hurt herself for making him a grey and wrinkled shadow of his former self. She nearly had been sick after that, had retched over the bathroom sink for a good ten minutes, tears tearing down her face. She'd had her first cigarette in seven years that afternoon, ashen at his kitchen table, rattling off a panicked monologue. He had just sat and listened to her, his hand around hers, stroking her thumb with his.

"Please don't try and say it's ok, because it's not. Don't try and tell me it's ok and it's going to be ok, and—"

"I wasn't."

A pause.

"I love your hands."

Nails bitten to the quick, dry and chapped from years of being dipped in acidic stop baths. She'd pulled her hand back, protested, laid bare all the faults she could possibly have found in her fingers. And still he smiled. And somehow, it was ok.

The first fuck. The last fuck. The fact that they are never going to fuck again goes screaming through her head. She hates the word fuck. It's his word, not hers: one of the many, infuriating bits of him that have seeped into her speech.

"Don't you love me?"

Not, "I love you", but "Don't you love me?", a question blurted out half jokingly on a lazy afternoon in bed. She'd never expected him to pause; to stop; to take breath. Ok, it was never voiced, but it was surely a given; an understanding; a mutually unspoken fact?

"Em, I care about you enormously—"

"But you don't love me."

"Don't be like that."

"Be like what?"

She knows what she's being like. Her jaw is clenched, her teeth are tensed, her voice is a hard little bullet inside her oesophagus. She kicks back the hotel duvet and furiously busies herself with her underwear. If she stops, she's going to cry.

"Like this. Get back into bed."

"You're the one who made this happen, Rich. You brought up sex, you brought up love—"

"When did I bring up love?"

"You said you loved my hands. 'I love your hands', you said, 'I love your body', 'I love being with you'—what, you love all those things and you don't love me? This was your idea, you're the one who made it ok for us to be doing this."

"Made it ok? Who do you think I am—God giving you permission to fuck about?"

"Fuck about?"

A guilty pause. She is paralysed, half dressed, looking back on him in the grimy hotel mirror. It has other people's fingerprints. Swimming in the duvet, she can see him trying to grab hold of the appropriate phrase, the appropriate placation, the apology that undoes that last horrendous phrase.

"That's what this is to you? A fuck while Magda's out, no strings attached?"

"Of course not." He's getting up now, struggling into trousers. "Of course there are strings."

"STRINGS? You're my husband's friend. I do yoga with your wife. Our kids go to school together. Of course there are fucking strings!" She's screaming and she knows it, she can feel the red in her cheeks, the undulating anger in her throat, raw as if someone had just scraped a grater down its length.

"Emilie, can you try to be coherent?"

"I am no longer coherent Richard, I am lying in pieces all over your bedroom floor."

A lazy afternoon in bed. The last lazy afternoon in bed. How different it might have been if she'd known then that that would be the last time they kissed, the last time she got to lie with her head on his arm, the last time they smoked illicit cigarettes and sprinkled ash recklessly on someone else's duvet.

A new theme tune starts downstairs. Half term. The park had been heaving. Everywhere middle-class parents frantically bribing their kids into good behaviour with McDonald's lunches and over-priced Mr Whippy's. She cannot believe she dragged the kids into this, her stomach shrinks at what they might have overheard, what they might have seen. Her head bangs against the cold, hard tiles. She is not this person. She would not jeopardise her family for nothing. And that's all it is: nothing. Something that might have been something once, but now in the midst of children and marriages and work and mortgages, estate cars, obligations and DIY, can never be anything. It hurts. She hugs her knees so tightly that they hurt. The tighter she hugs, the less she has to think: but the less she thinks, the louder the voices crank in her head.

"Magda knows."

She's been expecting him to want to make up, to apologise, to get back to normal: she wasn't expecting this. This news comes like a punch in the stomach, she can feel the blood draining from her face. Cool to a fault, even he looks on edge. He has a few days stubble on his cheeks, his eyes look a little tired, she longs to kiss his lids and feel the eyelashes flicker beneath her lips, but—

"She found the Polaroid."

The Polaroid. How stupid, how incredibly stupid, does a married man need to be to take a photo with his girlfriend? Very stupid. Stupid and drunk on an old bottle of vodka found in the chemical cupboard of his married-girlfriend's studio on a grey December afternoon. Shutting her eyes, she can remember the smell of the chemicals, the silence, the jump in her stomach when he'd appeared out of nowhere and put his hands on her hips. He was a good sport, he played along, poring over SLRs and wide angle auxiliaries, but the photos were just photos. "*I could do that!*" he proclaimed, bottle in one hand, her in the other. She'd laughed, laughed hard, laughed until she was curled over at the idea of him trying to take a decent photo.

It had really irked him, made his jaw tighten. He'd hated the idea she thought there was something he couldn't do. Everything was a competition, and he wanted to win in every category, photography included. Even red-cheeked and tipsy, she'd drawn the line at him using her proper cameras, reassuring now to think she had drawn some lines. She'd tried to fob him off with Toby's digital, but determined to triumph over everyone, everything, her, David Bailey, and Toby's technology, the very least he would settle for was a Polaroid. The battle to take the damn thing was a scramble, trying to pin her down to a suitable pose, implicitly sexual. The chase around her workshop produced half a dozen blurs and a fit of hysteria, the two of them playing younger than their children. It was only when her phone went off that the spell was broken. Harsh peals came like a knife slicing through the air, slicing through the suspended world of fun and make-believe. Toby's usual afternoon call. To say hi, to say he'd pick the kids up, to say *Love you* and *What's for tea?* Richard was perfectly still throughout the call, head bowed. She was embarrassed by the domesticity, the dullness, the detail to which he was now so inappropriately privvy. The *sweetness*, she knew he'd call it *sweetness* with a sarcastic grin, of a husband who called at the same time every day for absolutely no reason. Toby was bright, chatty, talkative: a great day at school, 9B had really come on, a 71% average on their stats paper, and all the time her insides were caving in, caught between two different worlds, two different men, the two different people she wants to be.

She'd hung up. Richard had picked up his coat, fanning the last photo in his hand. The two of them had watched in silence, foreheads touching, as their ghostly selves appeared out of the ether. "*Photograph means writing with light.*" As he waved it in the air, this stupid snap wrote out their story. It was mostly him, head thrown back in laughter, mouth open, rows of teeth. She was headlocked under his arm, a flail of hair, red painted fingernails gripping his jumper, half a corner of a smile all you could see of her face. He'd put it in his wallet: "*Something to look at over Christmas.*" And then he'd returned to his life, his world, his family for three festive weeks of turkey, in-laws, and BBC period dramas.

"She found the Polaroid. Don't worry, she can't see it's you."

"Oh thanks, I feel so much better."

He twists his hands, twists his wedding ring, the ring that's sat dully shining on his finger throughout all of this, just as her diamond has remained on hers, silently observing.

"I can't do this any more."

"What?" She stutters. His meaning is getting lost in the noise of the park. Children's shrieking is banging on her brain. He's mumbling into his collar, she can't hear properly, she's misunderstood.

"I can't do this, not now Magda knows. I can't lie to her face, Em. She's been so good about it—",

"Good about it?"

"—no threats, no divorce, no not seeing the kids. The only thing she wants is for this to stop."

Cold February air comes crashing into her lungs, reverberating around her rib cage. She is dizzy in the air and sinking into the ground. Life has come to a screeching standstill and all she can do is watch it. She's not participating any more. She can see her hands, her face, the angry tears threatening her eyes. She can hear a voice throwing his mess back at him, but it's not really her.

"Emilie."

◈◈◈

"Mummy?"

Alice, her five-year old shock of blonde hair and big eyes, is teetering in the doorway. Her thumb is in her mouth, her face somewhere between a smile and confusion. Mummy looks at her face in the mirror. Red puffy eyes squint out of a red puffy face, tears have made motorways all down her cheeks. The little girl clambers over her legs and throws herself down into a soul-consuming bear-hug. Somewhere near her shoulder the squeaky voice pops up: "What's for pudding?"

Pudding has to be found: tinned peaches rootled out of the back of a cupboard. Pudding, clearing, bathing. Telly off, pyjamas on, reading to Alice and trying to get Daniel to read to her. Somewhere in the middle Toby returns, brimming with apologies and causing two nearly-bedded children to hurtle downstairs like grenades launching into his arms. Standing on the bottom stair watching the three of them, she feels like a ghost. The banister beneath her hand is feather-light, the floor soft like candy-floss. She is floating with a half-smile and half herself.

More battle. Barbie versus Action Man as usual during teeth-brushing. Kisses and cuddles and arranging duvets, hanging up clothes, tidying toys, turning out lights. When she finally gets downstairs, it is to pasta bubbling in a saucepan and Toby, shoes, tie and jacket in the middle of the floor, clicking at the computer. She wants to tell him, to cry, to kiss him, to—

"Have you seen these photos?"

Her thought is broken. She is broken. "What?"

"The photos Daniel took today in the park. Some of them are a bit duff—" enlarging a muddy blur of green, "—but some are pretty good. Come look at this one."

His hand slips round her waist. She looks. She catches her heart in her throat. Yes, there's Alice being a lion in the foreground, yes, it's a lovely photo: but she is there behind her daughter, another man's hand resting on her knee. Toby is staring, grinning like a clown, but not seeing. Worse than his seeing is his not seeing. What is not seeing? Blindness, idiocy, oblivion. Yes, they're small, but how can he not see her head tilted towards him, his hand on her thigh, knuckles white even in the glare of the sunlight. How can he not see the pain, the tears, the anguish that is so stupendously obvious to her as to be palpable. Her finger glances against the hot, flat screen. A moment that can never be reconstructed.

Toby pulls her in closer onto his lap. Their faces are centimetres apart, she can trace the lines on his face with her fingertip. Her eyes brim again and she knows he sees.

"What?"
"I..."

I cheated on you. I cheated on you with your friend. I cheated on you in front of our children. I'm using the word cheat because I've made our marriage into little more than a game. I've forgotten everything that matters, or I've known and abused it anyway. I want to lie on the tiles of this floor and never get up. I want to sink into oblivion so I don't have to wake up next to you every morning and think about what I've done.

It's welling up inside her, she can feel it. Bigger this time, bigger than just tears or angry words. Bigger than storming out of an affair, bigger than taking two hours in a bathroom to cry about it. Something inside her stomach is surging towards her mouth, her intestines are twisting, hurling inside her. She's going to explode.

"I... I love you."

Three small pathetic words for one small pathetic person. So quiet, so nothing-like, so easily could they have been carried away by the wind or whisked off into the air. He looks at her quizzically.

"I love you too. Do you want carbonara or sundried tomato?"

Starting and Stopping

Eley Williams

IN FAIRNESS IT IS STILL about a week before she even realises that I am inside her. That is why she is carrying on the way she does; still jogging up and down these streets, taking in the washing, drinking red wine with her husband until all the lamplight splays and smudges, until the dining room ceiling falls around the bedroom floor. Once she twigs that I am on the cards I am sure she will be a bit more cautious.

I, of course, will politely bide my time. Not entirely idly either; I seem to have a whole lot of bobbing about to do.

◈◈◈

It is now a week later and, sure enough, there is the faintest, niggling suspicion in her mind that something might be up. *Something* being me, and *up* being – well, I am sure we will come to that later. She's leaning her forehead against a cooler patch on the bathroom mirror and counting on her fingers. Yes. Here we go: realisation taking hold. It would appear that 'niggling suspicions' are becoming concrete facts, slow understanding puffing up in little yellow pomanders in her brain chemistry. I will happily vouch for that last part being true because I can feel the imbalance of it in her bloodstream; there is not much I *can* do at present, but all these banging red swathes about me can communicate a great deal, if one only knows how to listen.

In all honesty, I am quite pleased with the gradual way she has cottoned on to me.

I reckon I have got 'niggling suspicions' down rather pat as a concept; 'niggling' is, after all, pretty much all I have got on my schedule for the next couple of months. As for 'concrete facts', I imagine I can only become one of those via a more thorough collaborative effort between her and myself in a few months hence.

◈◈◈

I have a feeling that I have started a little abruptly. Apologies: I would not wish to be unmannerly. (She would probably disagree on that last point as she bends over the lavatory again for the second time this morning because of me, but I digress). Maybe I have introduced the two of us too brusquely, in a strange mix of the impersonal and over-familiar; I know how to be very little else. I am a fast learner, however, and will attempt to do better. Therefore:

'She' is neither The Cat's Mother nor, really, One Who Must Be Obeyed. Names are important, the basis of communication, so I think it is right I should tell you 'she' is Laura. Laura is in her early thirties, blonde, five foot seven, nine stone five pounds, AB blood group, family history of Type One diabetes. Laura has a fondness for mint chocolates. Laura always wakes up at precisely 6.04am; she does not know why. I do, because I do not sleep. It is on account of the woodpigeons.

As for me, it is a month now since Laura realised *something* was *up*, and now she has a piece of paper from the doctor to prove it. She gets it out of the drawer in the bedside table from time to time. That piece of paper makes me feel like I have a receipt, and I do a little wary back-flip inside her every time she checks it.

She has not told her husband about me yet; I am a little concerned as to why. His name is Mark and he has the oddest effect on her pulse when he is with her. I should know: it is like being in a tumbledrier with a rattlesnake every time he comes in the room.

In other news, since realising that I am here Laura has started to try and eat well and has stopped jogging quite so often. Starting and stopping seems to be a pattern emerging in her habits: she has stopped drinking and smoking, started biting her fingernails. Stopped giving up her seat for others on the bus, started a new packet of After Eights.

◈◈◈

I had a picture taken of me today! At the doctors! Me, the little apostrophed nugget, caught mid-bob on a grimy piece of black and white paper. It looks a little bit like CCTV footage. Laura has put this picture next to my receipt in the bedside table. And has still not told Mark.

◈◈◈

I am getting more wakeful as time goes on; more wakeful, and more bored. I fancy I am turning into something of an industrious sort, so rather than fidget and make Laura all disagreeable I will try and describe where I am. It is snug, but huge; close, but cavernous. And the sounds of it! There is the heartbeat, of course, roaring away. But I can hear *everything*. The day she went to the doctors', for example, when they took the picture with their little ray gun, the sound of it was like wearing a mackintosh and feeling the rain upon you.

It is a fine line between cacophony and euphony in here: blood screaming down her veins, muscles twisting and twanging. When she blushes, there is a blue static all around me. Her breaths are a mad whale song; sometimes they rattle, sometimes grate, sometimes boom and creak. Everything quickening, everything thickening and it is all echoing about me as if her body is riddled with a biological tannoy system. Even her blinking can seem like timpani to me.

I wonder what noise I am making, or will make eventually. I try giving a little shout of her name, but the walls swallow it up.

◈◈◈

Not only am I more wakeful, I fancy I am getting bigger, too. As fat as a goldfish in here.

◈◈◈

I thought she was going to tell Mark about me today. She was eating some toast. Did I forget to mention the sounds of her eating? Such gnashing of teeth! The comedy spring 'Badoing!' noises in her throat every time she swallows, the weir and sluice sounds of digestion! Mealtimes are a matinee performance all of their own.

She was sat up considering him as he got dressed for work. I can tell she wanted to say something; I could feel all the sounds of her steeling herself. Laura steeling herself is quite a thing to experience. To be technical: her hypothalamus flares neon, her nicotinic and muscarinic receptors scream like foxes, her lacrimal glands tingle and start to slick over with a determined sheen of tears. We have had a lot of time together, Laura and I, plenty of time for me to anticipate and feel all these things as she does them. All the while her pulse was doing a little rumba number and, although she tried to make it as quiet as possible, for me the resolved clearing of her throat was like thunder and cannons in a wind tunnel.

Mark did not hear what I did, however. He gave her a peck on the cheek, did up his tie and was gone.

Her sigh made me somersault.

◈◈◈

Two months of me and, unexpectedly, Laura has taken up smoking again. I am a little resentful. She has also booked herself in for skydiving courses.

I do hope I am not making her impetuous.

◈◈◈

Now we are on the train and she is pressing her hands to her skin about an inch away from me. It is the first time I have been on a train and I am not too sure I like the movements of it. But Laura's colour is up. I enjoy that, at least. She seems to be looking for something.

There is a baby in the seat in front that keeps staring at her. She cannot help but look at it for the whole half-hour journey. Then, solemnly, she dips her head and crosses her eyes at the baby until it giggles, and spits a little, then giggles again and looks away. Mother and baby get off at the next stop and Laura watches their backs until the train pulls us out of sight. I am not sure what she is thinking right now, try as I might to focus in on her brain. There are suddenly too many colours there to make any one thought out.

Laura is clutching a list in her hand, clutching it so hard that not only is the paper crumpling but the ink is blurring in her hot palm, the words written there caterpillaring together into unreadable nonsense. Have I not mentioned the lists yet? There are now two lists next to my picture and my receipt in the bedside drawer. She has spent hours compiling them, the first covered with the names and numbers of people she needs to tell about me. This list is pleasingly long, but she was rather unsure of the spelling of some of the entries. The other list has the skydiving idea on it, and something about dolphins and sunsets. This list is numbered and the title is underlined twice. It is this second list she is holding now on the train.

She gets up with a sudden motion, swaying with the train, holding a grocery-bag full of After Eights. She is about to be rash. I can tell because blood is dashing in pinwheels about her heart in bright blue blazes. She is walking unsteadily up to an unknown woman by the train doors. I can tell this woman is unknown because Laura's brain is not accessing any memories as she looks at her. When Laura remembers, a spider-web of laser trails trace all over her mind, synapse connections pinging up acid yellow with information. It is quite a thing to watch; when she was compiling the list of names, her brain lit up like a cityscape at night. But there is none of that now: she has no prior memory of this woman.

The train is drawing in to our stop. She is telling this stranger that the stranger is beautiful. She is leaning in and, before the stranger can react at all, she has kissed the stranger. Then the train doors open and Laura is out on the platform. The train pulls away. And now she is alone with me, ticking off number 8 on the list and laughing like a maniac.

◈◈◈

Laura is telling Mark about me tonight. In a very roundabout fashion, if I may say so; apparently she has to admit to burning his dinner first. And how she never liked his mother anyway. And about the affair she had with the dentist last September. There was a little bit of crockery action at that. She then said her heart was breaking; it was not. It was as hot and full as I had ever seen it, and slamming the loudest tattoo against me in brandy-purple and butter-yellow beats. He held her by the hair for a bit, and shouted into her face. I quivered nearer to her spine and wondered why laughs and sobs sounded and felt so similar to me.

Then I came up as a subject, in a whisper, and there was quiet in the room. It was a quiet louder even than her heartbeat and I fancied I could hear the woodpigeons outside. I bobbed. She breathed.

Then he held her, and said words in her ear that brought the colour back to her face and to her fingers and to her lips.

"What shall I do now?" she asked, and her voice sent me spinning.

He did not say anything. She tipped her head upward, and tiny bubbles of air squeaked at the back of her throat.

"I want it out of me."

They spent the next hour in silence; I, literally bouncing with every movement of her diaphragm, her lungs, her heart, did not.

◈◈◈

I have not forgiven Laura for what she said to Mark that evening. I have been trying to ignore her, trying to stop sharing her feelings and savouring her movements as I get bigger. Sometimes I leak out little pangs for her to remind her that I am still here. Maybe that is malicious.

Anyway.

Laura is now at work. Or rather, at her place of work. She lectures History of Art at a university, where class has just finished with the drill of the bell. All the students have filed out and she busies herself picking up their detritus.

She stoops for discarded papers, she straightens to rub the whiteboard free of ink, she twists around to turn off the slide carousel. Then she pauses. The painting the class had finished with is still projected up on the screen, and she knows it well; I feel her brain accessing the information in a tickertape starburst of data: the title 'Adam and Eve' glows up in her memory, next to the date '1526'; this in turn sends neural streamers to 'Lucas Cranach', 'the Elder' and 'Oil on panel'. She has forgotten the height and width of the original; these facts are a hazier shade in the shadows of her mind and harder to make out.

She is in front of the projector now so that the painting plays over her flesh, the brushstrokes curdling over her face as she blinks in the light.

She is thinking about me.

I scramble, not relishing the attention. Laura reaches up at the slide, watching it bend over her fingers. She will reach for that doughy figure of Eve, I hazard. Or Adam, the two people who named everything. Names are important, the basis of communication. She will reach for either of these two and think of me, and her mind will be a firework display of secret neuron flashes that only my Laura and I will ever know about.

But she reaches up at the painting into something in the tree. Then the hand comes away, all thoughts stopped. I try shouting at her, but the vacuum made by her sudden stillness saps me of sound.

She picks up her pens and her laptop and her glasses and is out of the room without turning off the light.

◈◈◈

Mark and Laura have apparently decided to keep to their decision about me. They spend a lot of time on the phone and checking calendars.

Laura mentions to Mark the baby she saw on the train that day. She says it had a sweet smile and a very shiny head. She laughs. Then she runs her fingers through her hair, looking appalled.

And now they are joking nervously for a week.

◈◈◈

And now they are in the car. And now they are in the hospital. And now they are in a waiting room.

"I thought of naming it," says Laura. 'It' is me.

"How ghastly you are," Mark says gently, and kisses her hand.

"Apparently 'The Big C' is a popular name for it," says the receptionist, who had been eavesdropping. A filthy habit.

"The 'Big C'? The wide Sargasso?" barks Mark, and the two of them laugh. They are ghastly, they really are, cracking jokes that make no sense in a place that needs no jokes. Even the receptionist shoots them a look and goes back to her paperwork.

Laura is being brave, Mark is being brave for her and I am keeping very small, very quiet, and very, very angry.

A doctor comes with a wheelchair (as if I would cause Laura to need one! My Laura!) and she tucks herself in. Mark stands up. I wait, and listen to her breathing as the wheels and footsteps start up again and she is taken through the wards, past a hundred machines, a hundred buzzing lights, a hundred bald faces in beds.

Oncology, cancer ward, she reads from the signs to herself, and to me, as she passes through the final set of doors. Oncology, please turn right.

We turn right, and I feel her resolve getting stronger with each roll of the wheel.

Fellow of Queens' College, Cambridge, and a member of the Cambridge English Faculty, critic, poet and translator **Ian Patterson** has edited and translated Fourier's *Theory of the Four Movements*, and his translation of Marcel Proust's *Finding Time Again* (*Le temps retrouve*) was published by Penguin in 2003. He has published several books of poetry, and his *Time to Get Here: Selected Poems 1969-2002* was published by Salt, also in 2003. His most recent book is *Guernica and Total War* (Profile, 2007).

Nadia Connor is a second-year English student at Pembroke College, Cambridge. She lives in Sheffield.

Adam Crothers was born in Belfast in 1984 and is an English graduate at Girton College, Cambridge, writing a PhD dissertation about rhyme. His poetry has won the Quiller-Couch Prize (2005) and the Brewer Hall Prize (2007), and was longlisted for the Bridport Prize (2007). This is his second appearance in *the Mays.*

William Crouch is a third-year Philosophy student at Jesus College, Cambridge. He enjoys adventure, attempting to play jazz saxophone and being naked whenever legally possible. His creative output averages at one to two poems a year. He would like to improve this figure.

Ushashi Dasgupta is in her first year as an undergraduate at Oxford. She reads English at Trinity College. She has spent most of her life in Hong Kong, and has also lived in India and the United States. This is her first publication.

Megan Davies is currently studying Veterinary Medicine at Cambridge University. She enjoys drawing and painting and her favourite subjects are animals. Her small format art is held in private collections around the world.

Naomi Grant is a 3rd year English student at Jesus College, Cambridge. She is a student of the painter Israel Zohar in London.

Jane Han is currently reading English as an MPhil student in the Criticism and Culture program at Cambridge. Born in Ontario, Canada she completed her undergraduate degree at Princeton University where she was awarded the Martin A. Dale Scholarship for creative merit. In her younger, more naive years, she worked at United Talent Agency in Los Angeles fetching shoelaces for Marty Bowen (cf. *Devil Wears Prada*). She will be continuing her creative endeavors at Oxford next year where she will be attempting to "find the logic of it all" while pursuing a PhD in Fine Art.

Ian Heames studies English at Gonville & Caius College, Cambridge.

At the time of writing **Owen Holland** was a third-year English student at St. Catharine's college, Cambridge. He has been involved in an actor's capacity in numerous dramatic productions during the course of his time at Cambridge and, when there's time, tries his hand at various forms of cultural production, including photography, poetry and song. You can listen to the music at www.myspace.com/errantband. He had a couple of photos published in the Mays back in 2006; this is the first poem.

Simone Kotva was born in Stockholm in 1988. She is a first-year theologian at Emmanuel. As well as her life-drawing she also sculpts and has run the *Orpheists*, the Emmanuel College creative writing society. She enjoys going for walks in the snow.

Hazel Lambert is a finalist geographer at Newnham College Cambridge. Under the alias Hazel Hancock (HaHa) she typically frequents Balls, Events and parties as an on-the-spot caricaturist. This piece is one of her first forays in photography. Her main portfolio consists of mixed media explorations into how the form and surfaces of the human body form can be found mimicked in organic nature. Other achievements include setting up the now annual Newnham College Art Exhibition.

Christopher Morley completed his M.Phil. in Landscape Archaeology at Keble College, Oxford, this summer. When his bank manager has stopped threatening him with a large mace he would hope to return for the D.Phil. Outside of studying, he works as a professional field archaeologist. Writing is his passion and he is currently halfway through a novel (which, if nothing else, he will enjoy reading himself). This is the second of his short stories to be selected for *the Mays*, his piece 'The Changing Room' having been published in last year's volume. His other publication to date is an academic book review published in the *Archaeological Review* from Cambridge this year. Otherwise he has been slammed by Anne Robinson and voted off first on the Weakest Link. His other interests include sharks and dinosaurs.

A native of Mississippi, **Benjamin Morris** (Clare Hall) is a PhD Candidate in Archaeology at Cambridge. His work has been published and won recognition in both the US and the UK; this is his second appearance in *the Mays.* His preferred drinks is bourbon and rocks.

Marcelle Olivier is completing a DPhil in African rock art at Keble College, Oxford. She has published both poetry and short fiction in various South African and British journals and anthologies, and is currently working on a collection of poems on the theme of archaeology and anthropology. She is raising two cats named Juno and Mufti with her partner.

Beatrice Priest is studying for an MPhil in European Literature and Culture at Emmanuel College. She spent last year as Artist-in-Residence at Christ's College and is currently preparing for a second solo exhibition at New Hall in November. Her work concerns the representation of the female body.

Cortland Rankin grew up in Dallas, Texas and received his BA from Northwestern University in Evanston, Illinois in June, 2007. He began photographing extensively while at Northwestern, making frequent forays into the city of Chicago. Two of his urban portraits were recently honored in the Kiwanis Club of Evanston's 3rd Annual "Faces of Evanston" contest held in May, 2007. He is currently an MPhil student at the University of Cambridge in the Screen Media & Cultures program. Upon completion of this course in June, 2008, he plans to return to Dallas, where he will begin a teaching fellowship at his alma mater, Greenhill School.

Emily Tesh is a former Foyle Young Poet of the Year and her poems have appeared in *Magma and Mimesis.* She also co-edits *Pomegranate* (www.pomegranate.me.uk), a poetry ezine which aims to promote and encourage new young poets. Paradoxically, she generally prefers to read extremely old poetry and therefore studies Classics at Trinity College, Cambridge.

Francesca Whitlum-Cooper is a second year English student at Emmanuel College, Cambridge. She lives somewhere in between London and New York, and earlier this year was a finalist in the Glimmer Train Press' Short Story Award for New Writers across the pond. She is thrilled to have a second story published in *the Mays*, after her story "Last Words" appeared in last year's anthology.

Catherine Williams studies veterinary medicine with art on the side. Previous work has included public and private commissions displayed in Selwyn College and London and Cambridge galleries, backdrops for theatre, a 21 metre mural and hummingbirds on T-shirts. She has also illustrated for student publications in Cambridge and Oxford.

Prior to studying English at Selwyn College, Cambridge, **Eley Williams** won the nation-wide 'Christopher Tower' poetry competition in 2005, judged by Philip Pullman and Gillian Clarke. Two years previously she was awarded the 'Top Candidate' GCSE mark in the county for English, chosen from 957,620 entrants. These accomplishments, in addition to writing and performing for Footlights and the Recorded Drama Society while at Cambridge, pale in comparison to the fact she can whistle and hum at the same time.